Public Speaking in a Multicultural Society

The Essentials

Larry A. Samovar
San Diego State University

Edwin R. McDaniel
Aichi Shukutoku University

D0024447

OXFORD
UNIVERSITY PRESS

OXFORD

UNIVERSITY PRESS

Oxford University Press, Inc., publishes works that further Oxford University's
objective of excellence in research, scholarship, and education.

Oxford New York
Auckland Cape Town Dar es Salaam Hong Kong Karachi
Kuala Lumpur Madrid Melbourne Mexico City Nairobi
New Delhi Shanghai Taipei Toronto

With offices in
Argentina Austria Brazil Chile Czech Republic France Greece
Guatemala Hungary Italy Japan Poland Portugal Singapore
South Korea Switzerland Thailand Turkey Ukraine Vietnam

Copyright © 2007 by Roxbury Publishing Company

First published by Roxbury Publishing Company
Published by Oxford University Press, Inc.
198 Madison Avenue, New York, New York 10016
http://www.oup.com

Oxford is a registered trademark of Oxford University Press

Library of Congress Cataloging-in-Publication Data available

ISBN 978-0-19-533022-9

Contents

Preface

The traditional function of a preface seems to be two-fold: to state the purpose of the book and to describe the central features of the book. *Our purpose, stated optimistically, is to help you become a more effective communicator in what has become a multicultural society.* To accomplish this objective we have tried to cover those principles that apply to the type of public speaking situations that you are apt to face in today's increasingly multicultural world.

Rationale

The freedom to speak, and the ability to speak well, has long been recognized as both the duty and a requirement for all citizens of a democracy. In the United States, even the success and failure of your personal and professional relationships are often linked to your ability to speak well. In the last few decades, because of dramatic changes in the ethnic and cultural composition of the population in the United States, much of that speech is aimed at people from different cultures. The requirement to communicate across cultures has also increased as a result of growing international contact. More and more people are traveling to other nations, for both professional and recreational reasons. Hence, success as a communicator now demands that you learn to adapt your message to diverse audiences. This book seeks to assist you in mastering the speaking techniques that are instrumental in realizing that success.

Approach

Our approach to teaching public speaking is reflected in three fundamental ideas. First, we contend that communication is a social activity—*it is something people do.* Because it is a behavior we have approached the topic of communication from a practical point of view.

Therefore, we have placed in this book information and advice that is immediately useable—*ideas that can be translated into action.*

Second, our approach is also noticeable in the size of this book. That is to say, we have endeavored to be brief. We believe that you need to have time to prepare and practice your speeches in class. So while we have included information on speech theory when necessary, we also recognize that your communication class is the place where you actually engage in speechmaking. Furthermore, we hope that the succinctness of our material will afford the classroom instructor greater latitude in his or her explanation and application of speech principles.

Third, the contents of the text reflect our approach. To the extent possible throughout the book, we have mixed multicultural and domestic diversity illustrations with the more traditional public speaking examples. Additionally, references have been held to the absolute minimum. Instead, we have drawn on our personal expertise acquired over many years teaching public speaking and considerable experience in preparing and giving presentations to corporate and governmental audiences, both domestic and international.

Organization

Determining the sequence of chapters in a public speaking book is always a difficult assignment. Imagine for a moment the difficulty of deciding what you need to know first and what can wait until later. Because this book, and most likely the course you are enrolled in, is introductory, we decided to move through chapters in a way that progresses from the simple to the complex. Acquiring information in manageable increments will enable you to move smoothly from material that you feel comfortable with to more advanced principles. It is important to keep in mind that you need to take the accumulated learning from one experience to the next. In short, *each chapter builds upon the preceding chapter.* You cannot overlook information about gathering evidence or introductions and conclusions before arriving at the chapters on informative and persuasive speaking.

Chapter 1 begins by reminding you of the importance of communication, before moving to a discussion of the communication process. You are then introduced to the role of culture in the communication process—be it as speaker or listener. Chapter 1 concludes with a discussion of the fear of public speaking, commonly called communication apprehension, and offers ways to manage and overcome the condition.

Chapter 2 seeks to give you the information you need to "get started." The chapter introduces you to speech purposes, topic selection, methods of speech delivery, and note taking. Chapter 3 examines the process of audience analysis. The recommendations focus on individual, group, and cultural differences. Methods for analyzing the occasion are also offered.

Chapter 4 explains the various forms of evidence needed to prove and clarify your ideas. The discussion includes methods for testing the validity of the evidence and for integrating it into an actual speech. The chapter also contains recommendations that explain how to locate and record evidence for use in the speech. Sources as diverse as interviews and the Internet are scrutinized.

In Chapter 5 the discussion focuses on the proper ways to organize materials for oral presentations. Chapter 6 concentrates on visual aids—from the simple (posters) to the complex (using computer graphics). We look at what the most appropriate aids are and how best to prepare and present them.

Chapter 7 deals with speech delivery, offering suggestions for the proper use of both your voice and body. The chapter also provides information on how culture influences nonverbal behavior and presents recommendations on how to adapt your delivery to a multicultural audience.

Chapter 8 extends the theme of organization by looking at the subject of speech introductions and conclusions. Chapter 9 concentrates on the speech to inform. Here you will be advised on how to prepare, organize, and deliver informative speeches.

You will learn in Chapter 10 about persuasive speaking and how to present speeches that attempt to convince others to change their attitudes or behavior. The chapter highlights the value and use of evidence, emotional appeals, and credibility and offers recommended organizational formats.

The initial section of Chapter 11 explores language usage, including the role of culture, followed by a presentation of various devices for making language clear and vivid. The chapter concludes with an examination of ethics in communication. The ethical responsibilities of both speaker and listener are described.

Philosophy

Three philosophical premises have guided us in the preparation of this book. First, we believe that all individuals need to know how to speak well. We hold that a crucial and clear link exists between communication and a free society. In fact, at the core of democracy is the idea of citizen participation, and we want to help you improve your ability to participate. Second, as we noted early in the preface, communication is something you do—an activity. Hence, we believe that with knowledge and practice you can improve the manner in which you engage in those activities. Finally, we maintain that the study of public speaking does not start and end with a single course or with the reading of a single textbook. The study of communication is, indeed, a lifetime endeavor. We would therefore urge you to seek out as many opportunities as you can to practice this important art. Each time you wish to share an idea or a feeling with another person you face a new communication situation, the results of which should teach you something about the principles of social adaptation through speech.

Larry A. Samovar
Edwin R. McDaniel

Chapter 1

Communication and Culture

The Basic Concepts

"Why do I have to take a public speaking class if I'm not a communication major?" is a common lament of college freshmen. Well, there are at least three good reasons to do so. First, communication is necessary to function in society. Second, the U.S. democratic process relies on an oral tradition. Third, globalization and expanding information technologies are making our world much smaller, putting you in contact, both domestically and internationally, with people who communicate differently than members of the dominant U.S. culture. These events have increased the need for everyone to become a better communicator.

The chances for your success as a speaker are greatly improved by acquiring some specialized communication skills. These skills are so essential in today's society that most universities and organizations offer students and employees courses in effective communication. They do so because learning about communication instills an ability to think critically, solve problems, manifest high levels of personal credibility, adapt to social changes, develop self-confidence and poise, present creative and important ideas, and communicate interculturally. The main point should be clear: *Without communication skills we are unable to share thoughts and feelings with others.*

Because of this ever-increasing importance of communication and because communication can be improved, we have written this book to show you how to become a better communicator. This text is primarily concerned with how to effectively share opinions and ideas

1

with people from other cultural backgrounds. First, however, you must understand the processes involved. Therefore, this initial chapter examines what communication is and how it works, discusses the ways communication and public speaking are both alike and different, looks at the interface of culture and communication, and explains how to overcome the fear of speaking before an audience.

The Importance of Communication

Communication is an integral part of daily life. Indeed, an argument can be made that every waking moment involves communication. Even when not communicating with another person, you are engaged in a variety of intrapersonal communication activities, such as watching TV, listening to music, reading ads, determining when to change lanes on the freeway, deciding whether to go to class, and so on. A communication act can be something as seemingly inconsequential as complimenting someone on his or her appearance or as important as explaining symptoms to medical workers during an emergency. Regardless of the level or type, a communication act always has a consequence. Another important consideration is that because communication is a social activity, it can be changed—people can increase and improve their communication skills. This book is designed to help you achieve those two objectives in a way that benefits both you and the people you interact with.

The ability to communicate effectively is indispensable in professional life and a commonly specified employment prerequisite. This requirement has become even more salient as the United States moves from a manufacturing to a knowledge-based economy. Workforce diversity and globalization have introduced an additional factor—you must be able to communicate competently with people from many different cultures.

Communication is also important in social relationships. People engage in interpersonal communication for a variety of reasons—including entertainment (telling a funny story), therapy (complaining about a difficult exam), emotional expression (telling someone you love them), and explanation (revealing the reasons behind our actions). Your relationships will be more rewarding if you have the ability to communicate effectively. Knowing how to listen and to talk in a sincere, skillful manner to a family member, a close friend, a work associate, or someone from another culture can be beneficial to both parties.

The Communication Process

To understand the nature and function of speech, we must first examine the process of communication, of which speech is but one aspect. This text uses the terms "communication," "speech communication," "public speaking," "oral communication," and "speech" interchangeably, because a speaker is primarily engaged in communication whenever he or she, consciously or unconsciously, affects the behavior of others.

People ask and answer questions, take part in conversations, exchange ideas in meetings, participate in class discussions, and deliver formal and informal presentations. In every case, factors such as culture, credibility, interest, motivation, organization, listening skills, clarity, feedback, and delivery come into play. For example, although usually only one person talks during a public speaking event, the "other person" (i.e., audience members) is still sending messages. Nonverbal communication is present in all public speaking situations, and the way the audience responds is a type of message.

Defining communication is an assignment analogous to having to explain to someone why you love him or her. In both instances, it is often easier to remain silent and hope that you and your partner share similar meanings. The difficulty in both instances is that definitions of concepts as complex as love and communication are bound to be incomplete. The reason, of course, is that both can take many forms. But for our purposes, we can use a simple, straightforward definition. *Communication is the process of one person sending a message that creates meaning in another person.*

A key word in this definition is "process," which implies an interaction consisting of parts. Understanding these parts, or components, of the communication process is a prerequisite to becoming an effective public speaker.

The Components of Communication

The process of communication requires you to simultaneously manage eight important structural components. The first and most obvious component is the **sender**—the individual or group originating the message. In public speaking, the sender is the person who has a need or desire to communicate with others. To fulfill this motivation, the sender prepares and transmits the message to the receiver(s).

The **message** contains the information the sender desires to have understood. Messages take the form of verbal or nonverbal behaviors, which are encoded and transmitted via a channel to the receiver. The **channel** is the method used to move the message from the sender to the receiver. The message may be transmitted through a direct channel or may be mediated. For example, an oral message can be sent directly when in the presence of the receiver or can be mediated through a cell phone, radio, or television broadcast when at a distance. A visual, or nonverbal, message can be transmitted by waving good-bye to a friend as you drive away or can be mediated through a video camera or a photograph.

The **receiver** is the intended recipient of the message and the one who interprets the message. Because the receiver assigns a meaning, which may or may not be what the sender intended, communication is often said to be *receiver based*. If you tell your audience that the next meeting will start at four o'clock, most members will probably understand that you mean in the evening. However, someone may misinterpret your message and show up for an early morning breakfast meeting. After interpreting the message and assigning a meaning, the receiver may formulate a **response.** This is the action taken by the receiver as a result of the meaning he or she assigns to the message. In public speaking, the response is not usually immediate. Audience members will usually wait until the presentation is over before asking questions or making comments. The audience's response may also come later, depending on the speaker's message. Audience response can take many forms, such as voting for a political candidate, changing diets, or purchasing a particular product.

Feedback is another important component of communication related to, yet separate from, the response. Feedback is what allows the speaker to assign a qualitative evaluation to the effectiveness of his or her message. Perhaps the audience will smile and nod their heads, frown, or look confused after decoding the speaker's message. This behavior provides a clue as to how the message has been interpreted and facilitates adjustment of speaker behavior. Depending on the feedback, you may rephrase or amplify your message to provide greater clarity, or even retract the statement.

Every communicative interaction takes place in both a physical and a social **environment.** The physical environment is the actual place where the communication takes place, such as a classroom, conference room, or restaurant. The contextual, or social, environment is more abstract and influences the style of communication used. Think about the different communication approaches for conducting an interview, asking a friend for a favor, visiting your professor during office hours, apologizing for being late for a date, giving a presentation to a group of close friends, or addressing a large audience where you know very few of the people. People vary their communicative style in response to the occasion—the contextual or social environment.

Noise, the final component of communication, refers to the various types of distractions that can plague any communication event. *Physical noise* is separate from the communication interaction and can take many forms, such as a skateboarder rolling past the open classroom door, a noisy air conditioner fan, static from the instructor's microphone, or your cell phone cutting out.

Noise that is intrinsic to the people participating in the communication episode can also take a variety of forms. Suppose that during a Friday afternoon speech class you find yourself thinking more about other topics instead of paying attention to your classmate's presentation. Maybe you had a disagreement with your significant other and are trying to think of a way to patch things up, or you are excited about plans for the weekend. Perhaps you are even worried about the speech you have to give in class next week. These are all examples of *psychological noise* that can affect your mental state and reduce understanding of your classmate's presentation. *Physiological noise* relates to the physical well-being of the people engaged in the communication activity. Being sleepy, hungry, or plagued by allergies will detract from your ability to understand a speaker's message.

The final type of noise is one common to intercultural communication and most likely to produce misunderstandings. For intercultural communication to be effective, the participants must use a common language, which means that one or more of the people involved may not be using his or her native tongue. Complete fluency in a second language is difficult to attain and somewhat rare. As a result, many people who use another language have an accent or sometimes misuse a word or phrase, which can make understanding the message more difficult. This type of distraction, referred to as *semantic noise*, also includes jargon, slang, and even technical or professional terminology (West and Turner, 2004).

Taken collectively, these eight components provide an overview of factors that enable and influence a communication encounter, be it interpersonal or public speaking. Also of importance is the role of culture in each component, which is especially influential in intercultural communication. To appreciate culture's impact on communication, we must first have an understanding of culture itself.

Culture

Like communication, culture has many definitions, most of which can be complex and abstract, attesting to the difficult of explaining this social concept. For purposes here, however, we propose a simple, more applied definition. Recall the first time you went to an ethnic restaurant. If you were given a menu, did you know what to order? If you were accustomed to using a knife and fork, were you comfortable with chopsticks? If you had only eaten cooked fish, how did you react to sushi or sashimi? Any one of these situations may have caused you some confusion and apprehension. But you probably encountered other people in the restaurant who exhibited no difficulty in knowing what to order or how to eat it. This was because the other people knew the proper rules for obtaining and eating the different types of food. Think about meeting someone from another culture for the first time. Did you know the appropriate greeting—shaking hands, bowing, embracing, or a kiss on the cheek? These examples suggest an easily understood definition of culture: *Culture constitutes the rules for living and functioning in a particular social group.* The rules differ from one society to another; to function and be effective in a particular culture, you must know the rules and how to apply them.

You began learning your own culture's rules and norms at birth and have continued to increase that cultural knowledge throughout your life. As a result, the rules and behavioral expectations are ingrained, enabling you to react to recurring social situations without thinking. However, when you enter another culture, with different rules, problems can arise, especially in communication situations.

Communication and Culture

Communication and culture are inextricably interwoven. The communication style of a social group is a function of its culture, while culture is formed and transmitted through communication. Why do Euro-Americans normally shake hands when meeting someone in a formal setting? How did they learn this behavior? Why do the Japanese almost never use first names? Where did they learn this? Why do Arabs stand so close to each other in interpersonal settings? When did they learn this? The answer to all these questions is the same. People learn the culturally appropriate and expected social deportment, or rules, through communication.

If the behaviors of people from diverse cultures differ, we should rightly expect their communication styles to also vary. These differences extend far beyond the obvious dissimilarities of language and encompass variances in both verbal and nonverbal communication. How communication is used, the style employed, and even when to communicate are all products of culture. And what works in one culture may not work in another culture. Indeed, in a cross-cultural exchange, the accepted, normal communication practices of one participant may even be offensive to the other person. In such situations, communication can be seriously impeded by a lack of cultural awareness. This text is designed to help you increase your awareness of different communication practices and learn how to be a more effective communicator in our ever-increasing multicultural society.

In addition to the considerations discussed earlier in this chapter, another factor can influence communication interactions, especially when giving a speech. You have probably had limited public speaking opportunities. Therefore, it is important to recognize early on that stage fright, or communication apprehension, is a common experience. It is, however, something that is easily managed, as we explain in the final section of this chapter.

Managing Communication Apprehension

Most Americans find public speaking to be an extremely stressful experience and many place it above fears related to flying, heights, snakes, or even death. There are no scientifically validated explanations for this fear, but it is certainly quite common. Media celebrities, politicians, public figures at all levels, and even rock stars must deal with varying levels of stage fright. Regardless of how much public speaking experience an individual has, occasions will still arise when he or she experiences a degree of apprehension before and during a presentation. Competent speakers have simply learned how to manage their fear.

Within the field of communication, this sensation of mental—and, on occasion, physical—anxiety is termed *communication apprehension*. What you may feel when giving speeches, especially at the beginning of the semester, is a mild form of communication apprehension. The psychological apprehension may cause you to fumble for words or forget to present a particular visual aid when needed, and the physical anxiety might cause increased sweating, nervousness, dry mouth, or even shortness of breath. These nervous feelings are no different from what is sometimes experienced during a job interview or when preparing to ask someone out for the first time.

Basically, speech anxiety is the speaker's mind and body reacting to the fear of having an audience negatively evaluate his or her message and delivery style. As with any task, no one likes to think he or she might fail or perform poorly, and public speakers are constantly faced with the uncertainty of how their ideas and presentation skills will be perceived by the audience.

People who come from cultures that do not have a rhetorical tradition or who have learned English as a second language may have increased levels of anxiety. Many Asian cultures do not value speaking skills and place greater emphasis on the ability to listen empathetically. Second-generation Vietnamese Americans or Korean Americans, for example, may experience speech anxiety because they have not been enculturated to value oratory skills. However, everyone who aspires to be successful in the U.S. dominant culture will have to learn to make presentations to groups.

This discussion of communication apprehension is not meant to be frightening or discouraging. We are simply trying to increase your awareness and understanding of the possible influence of the phenomenon. Most of you will probably experience minimal or no anxiety. Additionally, you can use a number of methods to overcome or lessen these feelings of anxiety. As you read about the following measures to combat speech anxiety, keep in mind that they should be implemented well before the time comes to actually present a speech. Waiting until the last moment will only increase your apprehension.

Prior to Speaking

1. *Develop a positive attitude.* Fear of speaking in public can become a minor phobia. One way to develop a positive attitude is by selecting a topic of personal interest. Having strong feelings about a subject is likely to instill a sense of confidence. However, if you choose a topic you dislike, the entire speaking experience will probably be disagreeable.

2. *Be thorough in your knowledge of the audience.* A familiarity with the composition of the audience can lessen uncertainty about how they may receive the presentation.

3. *Think of speech anxiety as short-lived.* Anxiety is often highest just before standing up to speak. A satisfactory speech introduction usually dissipates anxiety.

4. *Start preparation early.* Lack of preparation is a major cause of stage fright. Waiting until the night before the presentation to begin preparing a speech is a sure invitation to disaster.

5. *Rehearse the speech several times, preferably in front of others.* Also, try to speak extemporaneously. Attempting to commit every word to memory can contribute to speech anxiety.

6. *Inspect the physical environment where you will be speaking.* Prior familiarity with the actual setting helps reduce anxiety and aids in making any needed adjustments.

7. *Try to engage in some relaxing behaviors just before the speech.* Tension-relieving techniques include (a) walking around or doing isometric exercises to help release nervous energy, (b) taking deep breaths or yawning to increase your supply of oxygen, and (c) taking a drink of water to keep your mouth from becoming dry.

While Speaking

When it is finally time to give the speech, several behaviors can help you maintain control over anxieties.

1. *Use effective delivery techniques.* Hand gestures, shifting your posture, and moving about will help dissipate the natural tension and simultaneously reinforce the verbal message. If

you use visual aids, the physical movements involved in manipulating and gesturing toward the visuals can help reduce nervous energy.

2. *Make proficient use of your voice.* Too many beginning speakers talk too fast. A hurried pace signals nervousness, further contributes to anxiety, and detracts from the audience's ability to understand you. Slow down and pause often.

3. *Do not apologize for minor mistakes, just continue with the speech.* In most instances, the audience will not be aware of minor errors or an omitted illustration. However, if the mistake involves a major distortion of the facts, ethics demand that the speaker pause and correct the misunderstanding. Also, if a person's name or a place name is mistakenly mispronounced, a brief "sorry," followed by the correct pronunciation is appropriate.

4. *Remember that the audience will usually not know you are nervous.* Most of the symptoms associated with speech anxiety are not evident to the listeners. In reality, the speaker is usually the only one who knows. Do not add to the apprehension by thinking everyone else is aware of your stress.

Chapter Summary

Communication is one of the most important aspects of work and social life, and people spend the major part of their waking hours engaged in various communication activities. Globalization and increased domestic diversity have created a growing need to be able to communicate effectively. This text is intended to help you become a competent and ethical public speaker, especially in a multicultural environment.

In its broadest sense, communication is the process of sending and receiving messages. The process, however, can be divided into eight separate parts—sender, receiver, message, channel, response, feedback, environment, and noise. Semantic noise can be a significant detraction in intercultural communication.

Culture can be described as the rules for living and managing social interaction in a particular social group, and the rules will vary from one culture to another. Communication and cultural are intertwined, and each culture has its own set of socially appropriate communication protocols.

Fear of public speaking, or communication apprehension, is a common condition, even for experienced speakers. Although its causes are not fully understood, it seems to surface when a speaker is faced with an unfamiliar role in an unfamiliar environment before an unfamiliar audience. The key to controlling communication apprehension is to remove as much uncertainty and unfamiliarity as possible. Thorough preparation and practice, coupled with a good mental attitude, will help guard against the disabling effects of communication apprehension.

Concepts and Questions

1. How can training in communication help in your specific career choice?

2. How often do you communicate with people from cultures different from your own? What are those cultures?

3. When interacting with someone from another culture, do you ever notice any differences in their communication style? If so, can you describe the differences?

4. What do think are the major differences between public speaking and private conversation?

5. What do you find most troubling when you are asked to speak before a group in public?

Activities and Exercises

1. Prepare a two-minute talk to deliver in class that mentions the intercultural experiences you have had at work, at school, or during your travels. Tell the class what you have learned from the experiences.

2. Interview a member of the class. Try to gather cultural or ethnic information that will aid the other members of the class in getting to know your interviewee. In a 30-second speech, introduce the classmate to the entire class.

3. Bring a personal picture or object to class and explain how the item offers insight into your culture or ethnicity.

4. Give a short talk that discusses why you believe so many people have a fear of public speaking.

5. Interview someone who you believe is a good public speaker. Ask the person what measures she or he uses to cope with communication apprehension.

Reference

West, R., and Turner, L. H. (2004). *Introducing communication theory: Analysis and application* (2nd ed.). Boston: McGraw-Hill. ✦

Chapter 2

Preparing a Message

Getting Started

Communication can be considered to be "purpose driven" in that it is usually initiated because someone wants to achieve an objective. In public speaking, that purpose is typically to obtain a desired response from the audience. Thus, any attempt to address an audience without a clear idea of what you want them to learn or do is a difficult task. A good presentation has a unifying thread that weaves all the pieces together, and that thread is the preconceived purpose. Deciding on the desired audience response allows you to more wisely select the materials, organizational patterns, language, and delivery methods that will facilitate achieving the objective.

To help you with this unifying thread, this chapter explains the initial steps of speech preparation, which include (1) deciding on a topic, (2) narrowing the topic, (3) formulating a general purpose, (4) preparing a specific purpose statement, (5) selecting a title, (6) choosing a method of delivery, (7) using notes, and (8) practicing the speech.

Topic Selection

The first question confronting the speaker is often, "What shall I talk about?"; there are several ways of addressing this question. In many instances, a speaker is asked to talk on a specific subject, so the topic selection has already been done. If a history professor requests a speech on the contributions of 19th-century Chinese immigrants to California's economy, or your employer asks for a presentation on the company's policy on benefits for unmarried partners, your topic is already decided. In such cases, the initial task is to narrow the subject to fit the specific audience and the time constraints. On other speaking occasions the event dictates the subject—such as a rally for a political candidate, a toast at a friend's wedding, a eulogy, or a graduation ceremony. However, in most instances the speaker must select the subject.

Beginning speakers can find themselves overwhelmed by the prospect of having to select their own topic. Yet, if you slow down and reflect for a moment, the task of topic selection will not appear so daunting. Here are a few procedures to follow to help you make intelligent choices regarding the general subject of your speeches.

Use Personal Resources

Selecting a topic that is interesting—to both you and the audience—will make the task of researching and delivering the speech more enjoyable. The first step in this process is to review what you already know. Examine your personal interests, experiences, and convictions. Consider any special knowledge you have, places you've traveled, or jobs you've held. Many students find it helpful to start the process of topic selection by taking an inventory of their knowledge and personal beliefs. By doing so early in the semester, you develop a list of possible topics to draw on for future speeches. See Table 2.1 for a sample inventory.

Looking Elsewhere

In addition to personal knowledge, many other sources can provide possible speech topics. News magazines, newspapers, reference books, newscasts, and computer searches offer ideas related to current events. Questioning friends and professors can also yield useful topics. Most college campuses have a variety of activities that can help generate still other topics: Guest speakers, debates on controversial topics, cultural events, and so on are all rich sources of material.

The Internet is also an excellent resource to help identify and research a speech topic. The World Wide Web provides a host of subject-based search engines, with Google and Yahoo! being the most popular. Once you choose a general category, such as religion, search engines will list hundreds of subcategories, suggesting countless subjects from which to choose. The Internet also provides access to a wide selection of newspapers, magazines, and television

Table 2.1
Personal Topics

Personal Experiences	Personal Abilities
ethnic background	musical instruments
vacations	athletic
jobs	artistic
foreign travel	intellectual

Hobbies	Cultural Experiences
bicycling	Japanese tea ceremony
designing web pages	Bat mitzvah
skydiving	Ramadan
camping	Kwanzaa
acting	Navaho sand painting
calligraphy	Chinese New Year

Personal Knowledge	Beliefs and Attitudes
foreign language	sex and violence on TV
sign language (e.g., ASL)	public transportation
first aid training	cloning
physical fitness training	drinking laws
religious studies	genetic engineering
senior citizens	health care costs

stations. For example, *Newsweek, Time,* the *New York Times,* the *Wall Street Journal,* and all the major networks (e.g., NBC, CBS, ABC, CNN, MSNBC, FOX) can be accessed via the World Wide Web or through your university library's online databases.

Avoiding Problems

Not all subjects are suitable for public speaking. Five general classifications of topics do not normally lend themselves to effective presentations:

1. *Some topics are too technical for an audience.* For example, a speech detailing how DNA is altered in selected bacteria to produce novel aromatic polyketides for the pharmaceutical industry might be appropriate for a group of bioengineers,

but most audiences would find it confusing and, ultimately, boring.

2. *Some topics are too broad to be covered adequately in a single speech.* A presentation examining all the causes of global warming, including the 10 steps to reduce greenhouse gas emissions, is an example of a speech that attempts to do too much at one time.

3. *Trivial subjects are risky.* Shallow topics can be used in some humorous speeches, but adults should not normally be expected to listen to a speech on, for example, how to cook a three-minute egg or how to drive a car. There are also times when a technical topic can be superficial if presented to the wrong audience. A group of astrophysics professors would be unimpressed by a speech on the basic elements of Einstein's theory of relativity. With a trivial topic, the audience may feel the speaker is insulting their intelligence.

4. *Some topics are too personal for a public forum.* Confidential and intimate self-disclosure is ordinarily out of place in speaking to anyone other than a group of close friends. Most audiences would be uncomfortable, for instance, if a speaker were to discuss the personal anguish felt over a family member's struggle with drug addiction.

5. *There may not be enough material available on a subject.* Too often, speakers select topics that cannot be researched and developed because not enough information is available on the subject. Although it might be interesting to look at how the Central Intelligence Agency runs covert operations, if that information cannot be acquired, preparing an effective presentation will be difficult.

Narrowing a Topic

After selecting a general subject area, you must determine what aspects of that topic will be relevant to the audience and meet the twin demands of time and purpose. Regardless of the subject, the speech must have a central focus, a unifying thread. An audience does not expect, or desire, a broad subject to be covered in its entirety. Consider, for example, how much more manageable the subjects in Table 2.2 are after they have been narrowed.

Almost all of these focused topics could be narrowed even further. Time spent thinking carefully about the many aspects of a subject will ultimately lead to selection of a topic that will be stimulating to you and interesting to the audience.

Table 2.2	
Narrowing Topics	

General Subject	Focused Topic
Education	Multicultural education Special education in public schools Rising costs of higher education
Illegal immigration	Rights of illegal aliens Controlling illegal immigration Driver's licenses for illegal immigrants
Presidential elections	Mobilizing minority voters Multilanguage ballots The Electoral College
Asian Americans	Filipino Americans Vietnamese Americans Cambodian Americans
American Indians	The Navaho creation myth American Indian medicine History of the Cherokee Nation
Chinese Americans	Chinese American Nobel Laureates San Francisco's Chinatown Chinese ethic groups
Advertising	Cross-cultural advertising Subliminal advertising Pharmaceutical advertisements
Environmental issues	Advantages of recycling Acid rain Declining ocean fish populations
Religion	Islamic beliefs Jewish holidays Chaldean Christians

Formulating a General Purpose

A particularly important aspect of preparing a speech is determining the general purpose. Why are you speaking? In a broad sense, there are three general speech purposes: to inform, to persuade and to entertain. Because public speaking courses usually focus on speeches to persuade and inform, the speech to entertain has been excluded from this book. Later in the text, individual chapters (9 and 10) are devoted to in-depth analysis of speeches to inform and persuade. Therefore, here we will provide only an overview of the two types.

Speech to Inform

An **informative speech** is intended to increase the audience's awareness, knowledge, and understanding of a topic. Because the aim is to teach, the information is presented in an objective, unbiased manner. A teacher demonstrating the procedures of the Japanese tea ceremony, your instructor explaining the course syllabus on the first day of class, and a health care representative explaining a medical procedure to a new patient are all examples of informative speaking. How much new information the audience has gained at the conclusion of a speech is the litmus test of a speech to inform.

The following are examples of informative speaking topics:

- Population diversity in the United States.
- The effects of global warming.
- How to make sushi rolls.
- The workings of a hybrid-powered automobile engine.
- How to apply for student aid.
- Rural poverty in the United States.
- AIDS treatment in Africa.

In each example, the aim is to have the listeners acquire or improve on a skill or gain new knowledge. After the presentation, the audience should know something they did not know before the speech.

Speech to Persuade

A **persuasive speech** attempts to convince the audience to believe, feel, or act in a manner advocated by the speaker. Persuasive speaking can center on convincing listeners to discard old beliefs and form new ones, or it can further strengthen opinions already held. In some cases, the objective may be to motivate the listeners to take some type of action. Persuasive speech is used when asking for a raise, requesting a deadline extension, or urging someone to go on a weekend road trip.

Here are some examples of persuasive topics:

- Illegal immigrants should/should not be granted amnesty.

- English should/should not be made the official U.S. language.

- Medical marijuana should/should not be legalized.

- The police department should/should not double its multilingual patrol staff.

- Voter instructions should/should not be printed in multiple languages.

- Women should/should not be restricted from military combat units.

- You should avoid high fat diets to reduce your chance of heart disease.

The persuasive aim is obvious in each example. The speaker wants the audience to modify an attitude, an opinion, or a behavior.

Formulating a Specific Purpose

While the general purpose of a speech may be categorized as to inform, persuade, or entertain, the **specific purpose** describes the *exact nature* of the desired audience response. The specific intent is often contained in a one-sentence summary of what the audience is expected to know, feel, believe, or do by the end of the talk.

When the general purpose is to *inform*, the specific purpose might be:

- To have the audience understand the history of affirmative action.

- To have the audience understand the availability of campus healthcare services.

- To have the audience understand how to apply for student loans.

- To have the audience understand the concept of "face" in Asian cultures.

- To have the audience understand the steps for recalling a political officeholder.

If the general purpose is to *persuade*, the specific purpose might be:

- To get the audience to vote in an election.

- To get the audience to sign a petition to reduce student activity fees.

- To get the audience to adopt stricter recycling procedures.

- To get the audience to contribute money for famine relief in East Africa.

- To get the audience to support a cost of living raise for local sanitation workers.

When preparing the specific purpose, there are several important considerations. First, remember that a *well-phrased specific purpose contains a single central, distinct idea.* A specific purpose containing multiple points is confusing. Second, the specific purpose should be *worded in terms of the response desired from the audience.* Specifying the desired response reminds everyone of the presentation's objective. A typical specific purpose statement might say, "At the end of this presentation, I hope you will sign a petition to help illegal aliens legally acquire driver's licenses." Finally, the specific purpose should be *phrased as a definitive statement.* Questions can make good titles, but they do not clearly specify the desired audience response. A good way to begin preparing for a speech is to write out the specific purpose, which can then be used as a guide for gathering and organizing material.

Selecting a Title

Often you will be asked to provide a title for your speech. Ideally, a speech title should be (a) short, (b) provocative, (c) suggestive of your purpose, and (d) appropriate for the audience and occasion. A couple of examples will illustrate how these elements can be combined in a speech title intended to stimulate interest: A talk on the merits and shortfalls of affirmative action was titled "Affirmative Action: An African American's View." A presentation on world religions used "God Comes in Various Shapes and Colors."

Determining the Best Method of Delivery

There are four fundamental ways of presenting a speech: (1) reading from a manuscript, (2) reciting from memory, (3) speaking impromptu, and (4) using extemporaneous delivery. However, many speaking occasions call for a combination of two or more of these types. For example, a speaker might begin by reading an introductory quote from a manuscript and then adopt an extemporaneous style by relying only on notes.

Using a Manuscript

Speakers using a manuscript read directly from a prepared text. This style of delivery is essential and appropriate for occasions when speakers are accountable for their remarks and must be extremely accurate. For example, speakers addressing congressional committees usually rely on a prepared text. Other speakers who often depend on manuscripts include radio and television newscasters, high-level government officials, and scientists. The benefit of reading from a manuscript is that doing so ensures the content is correct.

This type of delivery also has a serious disadvantage. The speaker can become so focused on the text that he or she loses rapport with the audience. Reduced eye contact with the listeners and reading in an emotionless, monotone voice will result in an unnatural or "wooden" delivery. Also, because the wording and phrasing are decided in advance, a manuscript speech lacks flexibility. The speaker is unable to alter or adapt the text to the changing moods and needs of the audience.

If you encounter a speaking situation that dictates relying on a manuscript, remember to (1) write the speech for the listeners and not the reader, (2) practice reading aloud, (3) use eye contact and other techniques of effective delivery, (4) concentrate on getting ideas across, not just the words, and (5) use a clear, large font size that makes reading the manuscript easy.

Speaking From Memory

Much like a manuscript speech, a memorized speech offers the advantage of a carefully thought-out, well-worded presentation.

Every word is committed to memory, which requires considerable time and effort. However, this method often leads to a mechanical delivery style. A memorized speech is also dangerous because the speaker can easily forget something. It is usually difficult to remember exact wording, and if one word is forgotten, the speaker may not be able to recall larger parts or may even forget the entire speech. These disadvantages and dangers far outweigh any advantage of memorizing a speech. Thus, public speakers should avoid relying on memory to deliver an entire presentation.

Speaking Impromptu

Impromptu speaking is being called on to address an audience on the spur of the moment, with little or no advance notice or preparation time. Much of our daily conversation is a series of short, impromptu talks. The main advantage of impromptu speaking is that it is spontaneous, which makes it very natural. The chief drawback is lack of preparation, which often encourages a speaker to ramble. When facing an impromptu situation, (1) try to tie together all of your thoughts quickly—in a few seconds or minutes; (2) attempt to relate the topic to something you are familiar with; (3) organize your thoughts into an introduction, body, and conclusion; (4) be concise; and (5) stay on topic.

Using Extemporaneous Delivery

Extemporaneous speaking is by far the most desirable delivery form. It allows the speaker to prepare in advance, and has the advantage of "communication flexibility," because adjustments can be made *during* the talk. Extemporaneous speaking requires that a speech be (1) researched, (2) outlined, (3) practiced, and (4) delivered in a conversational manner.

Research. When you speak extemporaneously, you are aware of your presentation topic and purpose before hand and have time to gather the necessary supporting information.

Outline. After researching the topic, you organize and outline your data into a clear, systematic pattern. Normally, the outline will contain key words and phrases or a single, short sentence for each subtopic, all of which can serve as memory aids. The exact wording of the speech is not determined until the actual presentation. For an extemporaneous speech, *do not* write out the entire text; the temptation to read the text will be overwhelming.

Practice. Knowing about the speaking occasion in advance allows you to practice the speech. Do not memorize the exact language for delivery; instead, learn the organizational pattern, main points, sub-points, opening, and closing. When practicing, focus on ideas, not on specific words. Practice aloud and time the presentation to determine approximately how long you need for delivery.

Delivery. The delivery style for extemporaneous speaking is intended to be natural, unscripted, relaxed, and conversational in nature. Using only notes or note cards gives you a greater opportunity to establish rapport with the audience through directness, eye contact, spontaneity, and a general conversational tone. You can also more easily monitor and respond to audience feedback. For example, if the audience appears confused about a particular part of the presentation, you can stop and say, "This is an especially important point, so I want to explain it another way." The only significant shortcoming of the extemporaneous method is the time required to research, outline, and practice the presentation.

Although we've discussed the various methods of delivery independently, it is common to use two or more in a single speech. For example, a speaker may decide to use the extemporaneous method, but write down and read an important statistic, while committing a clever quotation to memory. A competent public speaker is flexible and does not rely on a single delivery style, instead adapting to the occasion.

Because this book focuses on speaking in a multicultural environment, we need to caveat our instructions on delivery methods. Much of what has been discussed about delivery is a product of the Euro-American tradition. Not all cultures would agree about the advantages of the extemporaneous style. For example, the Japanese and Chinese lack a rhetorical tradition and sometimes find direct eye contact uncomfortable in formal situations. For them, the manuscript speech is usually the preferred method of delivery. However, in Arab and Mexican cultures, where rhetorical artistry is an admired trait, most people enjoy speaking and are not hindered by impromptu situations.

Using Notes

The use of note cards has enjoyed a long history in public speaking courses. It is still common to see students stand up before their class with a handful of 3 x 5 cards, often overflowing with statistics, dates, quotations, even complete paragraphs, and sometimes the entire speech. Frequently, the audience must endure the speaker having to arrange and rearrange the cards throughout the presentation. This situation is a result of inadequate preparation.

You will *never* see note cards used in a professional presentation. The accomplished speaker will rely on a single note sheet placed on a podium or table, or more commonly, will use the accompanying graphics as memory aids. The advent of electronic graphics, especially Microsoft PowerPoint, has made written notes largely obsolete. With this trend in mind, we will discuss the use of notes in general rather than note cards specifically. We recommend you try to use note cards sparingly.

The reason for having notes is obvious—most public speakers simply cannot remember everything. Notes provide the keywords and phrases that trigger the speaker's memory and offer a safety net for those instances when the presenter draws a mental blank. The following suggestions will assist you in preparing and effectively using notes during a speech.

1. Try to limit written notes to a single sheet of white paper or a few 3 x 5 cards. (If you use note cards, number them sequentially in the upper right hand corner, which will help you keep them in order.) Always write on only one side of the paper or cards. Doing so allows you to horizontally slide the top sheet or card off the second one. Flipping cards will distract the audience.

2. Write down only what is needed to remind you of the main points and subpoints. Do not write out the entire speech—it will become too tempting to read to the audience.

3. Notes should be in an outline form and follow the same structure as the larger speech outline.

4. Write out any long quotations, expert testimony, or statistics. Even better, make a visual aid that displays the quotation, testimony, or statistics. The visual aid then becomes the memory aid.

5. Type or print notes using a font size that is large enough to be easily read when standing at a podium or table.

6. When practicing the speech, use the notes in the same manner as they will be used during the actual presentation.

7. Do not attempt to hide the notes. There is nothing wrong with using notes for a public speaking presentation, if you do so professionally and in moderation.

We have focused on written notes that are separate from graphic aids. However, it is becoming increasingly common to use visual aids as a prompting devise. The use of visual aids, which include transparencies, flipcharts, graphs, maps, posters, electronic visual displays, and computer graphics will be covered in Chapter 6.

Practicing the Speech

Without adequate practice, research and other preparation efforts will be for naught. Practicing helps you become more familiar with the material, helps you formulate different wordings for topics and subtopics, and provides a degree of self-confidence before stepping in front of the audience. Here are some guidelines for practicing a speech:

1. Have a positive attitude. View practice as an opportunity to develop and sharpen skills that will enable a smooth presentation and minimize personal tension.

2. Practice early and often. Begin at least three days before the actual presentation.

3. Start by practicing with the main outline. After you learn the key outline points, it will be easy to move to notes.

4. Work to remember ideas, not exact words.

5. Practice the complete speech at least three or four times.

6. Time the talk. This allows the addition or deletion of material to meet the allotted time.

7. Make the practice sessions as realistic as possible. Practicing a speech by "running it through your head" while listening to a favorite CD or watching *American Idol* will not be helpful when you encounter the actual speaking situation. Here are a few suggestions to increase realism:

a. Practice the speech standing up. Ideally, rehearse in the same room, studio, or auditorium where the speech will be given, or in a place that approximates the location.

b. Practice the speech in a realistic manner. Try to practice using the ideas and concepts you will use in the presentation.

c. Practice with the same memory aids (notes, outline) and audiovisual aids (posters, models, computer aids) that will be used in the final presentation.

d. Develop the habit of not stopping the speech when practicing aloud. When actually giving the speech, you will not be able to stop and start over every time you make a mistake or use the wrong word.

e. Try to rehearse the speech in front of an audience—your roommate, parents, fellow class members, or anyone who will listen. One communication study has confirmed that practicing a speech before other people will increase the speaker's performance (Smith and Frymier, 2006).

8. If possible, videotape a practice session and do a self-critique.

Chapter Summary

The purpose of public presentations can be grouped into three general categories—to inform, persuade, or entertain. In addition to selecting a general purpose, a speaker must formulate a specific purpose that describes the immediate and exact nature of the desired audience response. A good speech title is brief, appropriate, provocative, and suggests the purpose of the speech.

Any one of the following methods can be used to deliver a speech: (1) from a manuscript, (2) from memory, (3) impromptu, or (4) extemporaneously. The extemporaneous method is recommended for beginning speakers. When using notes, it is important to (1) keep them brief; (2) write out direct quotations, expert testimony, and statistics; (3) write clearly; (4) write personal reminders; and (5) practice with the notes. Speakers should begin practicing early, make the sessions realistic, practice in front of an audience, use video equipment if available, and allow time for a final run-through.

Concepts and Questions

1. What are some major considerations when selecting a speech topic?

2. What are the four main methods for delivering a talk? What are the advantages and disadvantages of each?

3. Why is practicing a speech such an important element to successful public speaking?

4. What are some guidelines in preparing and using notes?

5. What are the major differences between a general purpose and a specific purpose?

Activities and Exercises

1. Prepare a short speech on your main hobby or favorite activity. First, deliver the talk by means of a manuscript. Then change the speech so that it can be delivered extemporaneously. What major differences did you experience?

2. After delivering an impromptu speech in class, take the same topic and develop it into a more detailed extemporaneous speech. What differences did you notice in both content and delivery?

3. Formulate a general and a specific purpose for the following topics:

   a. Problems of domestic diversity.

   b. Advantages of globalization.

   c. Healthcare costs.

   d. Interpersonal conflict across cultures.

   e. Race relations on campus.

Reference

Smith, T. E., and Frymier, A. B. (2006). Get 'real': Does practicing speeches before an audience improve performance? *Communication Quarterly,* 54: 111–125. ✦

Chapter 3

Adapting a Message

Analyzing and Understanding the Audience

Soliciting and holding the attention of a diverse group of people is not a simple task. What interests one person may not interest another. An individual's reasons for believing or acting a certain way are the product of a wide-ranging variety of influences. Culture, race, ethnicity, gender, family, the neighborhoods one grew up in, the schools one attended, the groups one belongs to, and a host of other factors help produce an individual's unique outlook on topics. In short, people are the product of countless influences, and these influences shape their view of world. Because of these many and varied stimuli, it is necessary to adjust your communication messages to accommodate the diverse populations you encounter daily.

To illustrate this situation, reflect back on your high school days. Recall when you had to ask your parents for permission to do something—perhaps to attend an out-of-town rock concert with a group of friends. When approaching your father, did you use a different communication style and set of arguments than you used with your mother? From prior experience, you had learned to tailor distinct, separate messages that would appeal to each parent. The communication style used to persuade a close friend to help you move to a new apartment would probably be quite different from the one you would use to ask your employer for a day off. Depending on the social context, the participants, and the desired objective, people vary their communication in an effort to conform to the occasion.

This chapter is about adapting not to a single person but to an entire audience composed of many individuals. The basic premise seems rather simple—people are different and they are alike. As a public speaker, you must try to locate similarities among audience members if you are to achieve your communication objectives.

The Importance of Audience Analysis

In almost every communication encounter, the other person is taken into account and assumptions are made about that individual. For instance, in an initial encounter with a stranger, the first things we usually notice are their outward features—whether the person is young or old, male or female, Asian American, African American, or Euro-American, casually or formally dressed, and so on. A speaker uses these observations to adapt his or her communication style and messages to fit the receiver. As the speaker acquires more information, he or she makes further predictions about how the receiver might view the message and the speaker. When these same predictions and adaptations are made in reference to a group of people the process is considered audience analysis. **Audience analysis** *means learning about the people you are, or will be, talking to in order to adapt the presentation to their specific interests, needs, attitudes, knowledge, beliefs, values, and backgrounds.*

Audience Assessment

At any public speaking event, the audience consists of individuals, and just as no two people are alike, no two audiences are exactly alike. This reality requires the speaker to first obtain information about the audience and then allow this information to steer the speech preparation process.

The following list of questions, while not exhaustive, is meant to serve as a general guide for gaining insight about an audience. Answers to the questions will assist you in determining what information should be included in the talk and how to effectively present that information.

1. What is the audience's interest in the topic?

An effective public speaker must ensure that the audience is interested in the topic. Thus, it is necessary to gain an understanding of the listeners' background and select a topic that will appeal to their interests. The challenge of maintaining audience attention is greater when you have no choice in the topic selection. In those instances, the presentation itself must be tailored to solicit and maintain the audience's interest.

2. What does the audience know about the topic?

A topic presented below the audience's knowledge level runs a risk of being boring or even insulting. Alternatively, the topic should not be presented in a manner that greatly exceeds the audience's knowledge level. A speech on the basics of the Japanese tea ceremony given to a group of accomplished tea masters would likely be received as boring and perhaps even condescending. Conversely, a freshmen chemistry class would probably be confused by a talk on the theoretical computations of advanced physical chemistry.

3. What is the audience's attitude toward the topic?

What is the audience's opinion? Attitudes exist along a continuum from favorable to neutral to unfavorable. For a neutral audience, the speaker must find a way to elicit and maintain their interest in the topic. If they are favorably disposed to the subject, the task is made easy, but if they hold negative opinions, the presentation must be designed to overcome those objections. Suppose you are tasked to give a speech intended to get voters to support a state proposition allowing illegal immigrants to obtain a driver's license, but you find the audience is generally opposed to the measure. The speech would need to be tailored to talk less about the advantages immigrants would receive and more about how the audience members themselves would benefit from such action.

Listeners' Characteristics

A speaker must always realize that an audience is composed of unique individuals, and characterizations about that group will probably not apply to every member. The audience analysis should provide some general background information about cultural history, group affiliation, educational level, occupation, gender, age, and the like.

Used properly, this general information can reveal a great deal about the audience members. This usefulness is based on the assumption that as *members of a culture or group, listeners share a set of norms, perceptions, attitudes, motives, needs, values, and interests.* The speaker's job is to discover the listener's affiliations, make some valid generalizations about those relationships, and adapt the speech to accommodate those conclusions. In short, regardless of the audience or occasion, the question is always the same: What do the listeners bring to a speech that will influence how they respond to the speaker and the specific purpose? What listeners bring is both general and specific and falls into four broad categories: (1) *a fund of knowledge* (what they know about various subjects); (2) *attitudes* (their feelings about a topic); (3) *beliefs* (what they believe to be true or false about the world); and (4) *values* (how they believe they should act in the world). In each of these categories, an individual's culture exerts a strong influence. To better understand how this influence works, we will now look at a variety of cultural traits that can have a bearing on how members of an audience perceive a presentation.

Cultural Traits

The United States is currently experiencing dynamic and dramatic cultural changes. Technological advances in transportation and communication have drastically "shrunk" the world. Compared to 30 or 40 years ago, it is significantly cheaper to travel across the United States and quite affordable to reach international destinations. Modern telecommunications allows us to have frequent interactions with family and friends around the world.

The near-constant arrival of new immigrants is reshaping the demographics of the United States. Large populations of people from varied ethic and cultural groups now consider the United States to be their home. The previous historical and geographical experiences of these groups have caused them to perceive the world quite differently than do members of the dominant Euro-American culture. While the phrases "cultural diversity" and "global economy" are often overused, they do remind us of the notion that in all aspects of contemporary social life we are interacting more and more frequently with people whose cultural heritage is different from our own.

As we discussed in Chapter 1, culture can be readily defined as a set of rules that govern social interaction for a group of people. However, because of the increase in cross-cultural contact in the United States and the almost certainty of a culturally varied audience, we feel it necessary provide a more comprehensive discussion of the cultural factors that can influence your audience analysis.

Culture *has been described as the totality of learned and accumulated experience that is socially transmitted from generation to generation.* This rather dense definition is saying that culture instills in each of us, in both conscious and subconscious ways, patterns of behavior, thought, beliefs, attitudes, ideas, values, and many of our habits. To understand the people we communicate with, we must also be aware of the cultural characteristics they bring to a communication interaction.

However, two important points need to be made. First, we must be careful not to rely too heavily on preconceived notions about another's culture. All too often, those notions are based on limited experience and unrealistic images of a culture as portrayed on TV, in movies, in novels, and in the remarks of biased or unqualified observers. Moreover, we must remember that perceptions of other cultures might be influenced by a feeling of **ethnocentrism**, *which is a tendency to judge all other cultures by the standards set in one's own culture.* Ethnocentrism is dangerous because it can negatively influence one's collective perception of another culture or one's attitude toward an individual from another culture.

Second, we realize that the United States is composed of many cultures. However, when referring to the "dominant culture," we are talking about that segment of the population that enjoys the most power and influence. They control and dominate the major institutions (corporate, educational, and government) and determine the flow and content of most of the information (e.g., media outlets). In the United States, the majority of this power is currently held by what is commonly referred to as Euro-Americans.

American Dominant Values

The following is a brief summary of some key values as they apply to the dominant American culture. The list and discussion of these values will serve two purposes. First, it will help you understand members of the dominant culture and how to tailor material to appeal to those individuals. Second, the discussion will also serve as a foundation for understanding how values function in other cultures.

Individualism. Probably the most sacred of all American values is **individualism**, which refers to the idea that each person is unique and special. Most Americans believe that the interests of the individual are, or ought to be, paramount, and that all values and rights originate in individuals. Whether in ethical, social, or sexual matters, the self holds the pivotal position for Euro-Americans. This key value can be seen in a variety of daily expressions: "Pull yourself up by your own bootstraps" (initiative), "Rules are for fools" (independence), "My way or the highway" (self-expression), and "A man's home is his castle" (privacy). These beliefs need to be considered when preparing a persuasive presentation to an audience that values individualism.

Materialism. People in the United States also value materialism. They consider it almost a right to be materially well off and physically comfortable, and they often use material possessions to judge a person's success and assign status. The pursuit of material things is a driving force in the lives of many Americans. There is even a popular bumper sticker that proclaims, "Whoever dies with the most toys wins." Speeches for an audience with a strong materialistic mindset need to be crafted to demonstrate the material benefits to the individual.

Work. Hard work is an important value in the United States. Whether motivated by ego gratification, material possessions, or the Puritan ethic, Americans believe that work is important. When people meet each other for the first time, a common question is "What do you do?" Embedded in this simple question is the belief that "what we do" contributes to our personal identity.

Progress. In the name of progress, Americans emphasize adaptability, technological innovation, economic expansion, and change. Since the beginnings of the United States, people have railed against stagnation and the status quo. While conquering the land, seas, airways, and finally space, progress and change have been prime articles of faith for most Americans. They enjoy what is new and different. Each generation seeks to stake out new territory and contribute to change.

Democracy. While closely linked with the value of individual freedom, democracy is important enough to have its own listing. Since the nation's founding, aristocracy and authoritarianism have been rejected. From the Declaration of Independence to an insistence on majority rule, Americans pride themselves on being the most democratic people in the world. They believe that all people have a right to succeed in life, and that the state, through laws and educational opportunities, should support and encourage that right. The belief in democracy is so strong that many of our government policies are designed to promote democratic reform in other nations.

Competitiveness. The American dominant culture is marked by competitiveness. Whether in sports, business, or personal life, people are taught to strive to "be the best." The U.S. economic and social systems thrive on perceiving life as a contest that categorizes people as winners or losers. The slogans of two major U.S. corporations, "We're Number One" (Hertz) and "Just Do It" (Nike) emphasize how competitiveness permeates American society.

Cross-Cultural Values

The influence of culture on communication is of immense importance. Culture instills people with a worldview, which provides them a means for dealing with issues of life and death, suffering and happiness, heaven and hell, right and wrong. Culture also provides groups with certain ways of perceiving and responding to such events and ideas as work, leisure, violence, change, conflict, sexual conduct, gender, the elderly, and self-worth. How people view, accept, and enact these concepts varies across cultures. Therefore, the following pages provide a brief overview of those important cultural values and characteristics that should be considered when speaking to culturally diverse audiences. The list, not intended to be exhaustive, introduces the importance of understanding a person's cultural background in order to successfully accomplish the communication objective—be it informing or persuading.

Nature. The differences in conceptions of the relationship between humanity and nature and the environment produce distinct frames of reference for human desires, attitudes, and values. While some cultures believe that nature should be "tamed" and controlled, many others (e.g., Asian, American Indian) believe that people should live in harmony with nature. Their philosophy holds that a "power" links all things and creatures together. If a speaker gives a presentation to an audience composed of American Indians, in support of opening national forests to off-road recreation vehicles, he or she would need to explain how the operations would not exploit or despoil the natural environment. Talking from the Euro-American view that it is both a right and a mandate for human beings to control nature would be an unsuitable premise on which to base arguments for that audience.

Collectivism. As noted earlier, individualism is a strong personal value for most Euro-Americans. However, in the majority of the world's cultures, and in many nondominant American co-cultures, **collectivism** shapes a person's view of the world. Whereas Euro-Americans tend toward individualism, stressing self-motivation and competition with others, Eastern and Latin cultures give primacy to the group.

One result of collectivism is a strong emphasis on family. In the Middle East and Latin America, the family is seen as the most important social unit. Middle Easterners are so protective of their families that they would never berate a family member, even in jest, in the presence of an outsider. Moreover, if someone were to boast of being a "self-made man," it would be seen as an affront to the family—implying that the family had been derelict in its responsibility to the man. Hence, a speaker addressing a Mexican-American or an Arab-American audience might promote the benefit of a product or a particular course of action to families, rather than to the individuals.

Uncertainty. Cultures also vary in the amount of uncertainty and ambiguity they can deal with. People from cultures such as the Greek, Japanese, French, and Portuguese do not like the unknown, and they function much more efficiently when the uncertainties they face are minimized. In these cultures, there is a need for rules, a wish for specific proposals, a strong respect for the view of experts, and a dislike of risk taking or change.

Other cultures have a high tolerance for the ambiguous nature of life. People from Denmark, Sweden, Ireland, Great Britain, and the United States do not normally feel stressed when some issues are left unresolved. Knowing a culture's view of ambiguity can enable a speaker to decide how specific or direct proposals must be. A high-uncertainty audience will expect many more details about a proposal than low-uncertainty listeners, who will be more focused on the end result.

Formality. An audience analysis should also include consideration of how a culture values formality and informality. This variable has an impact on issues such as status, language, content, and delivery. For instance, the United States is characterized by a rather informal culture, while Germany, Japan, Egypt, and Great Britain are cultures where correct protocol and conventional behavior are expected and appreciated. In most formal cultures, one's last name and titles are used, dress style is conservative, and correct language is stressed. In the United States, where informality is valued, people normally move quickly to using first names and sharing personal information. Violations of the norms of formality and informality could well hinder a speaker from achieving the objective of his or her presentation.

Time. Cultures also perceive time differently. Whether or not a culture places emphasis on the past, present, or future will influence how people in that culture respond to messages and even how they will concentrate on the speech itself. For Euro-Americans, a future-oriented culture, what is yet to happen is of great importance. We are always planning and thinking ahead. We tend to believe that things will be better in the future.

Past-oriented cultures believe in the significance of prior events. History, established religions, and traditions are extremely important to these cultures, so there is a strong belief that the past should be the guide for making decisions and determining truth. This orientation is prominent among the Chinese, who, because of their long and splendid history, continue to respect the past. For the Vietnamese, reverence for ancestors is important, so the past remains paramount. The English, because of their extensive devotion to tradition, continue to resist change. Knowing how these three cultures venerate the past can help speakers prepare and present their arguments in a more credible manner. For example, when speaking to an audience of first- or second-generation Asian Americans, a culturally aware speaker would probably avoid saying that something should be rejected just because "it is old" or "out of date."

Credibility. Although a comprehensive discussion of speaker credibility will be presented in a later chapter, it is important to understand how significant cultural influences are in shaping an audience's view of the presenter. A speaker who is perceived as dynamic, outgoing, and articulate by an American audience will enjoy high credibility. Yet this same person is apt to be viewed as aggressive or presumptuous by an Indonesian or Thai audience. These cultures are more accustomed to a quiet, humble, pensive, reserved approach to communication. American diplomats and executives dealing with the two Southeast Asian cultures will attest to the advisability of downplaying the sort of demonstrations of enthusiasm and persuasiveness that are greatly admired by many Western audiences. On the other hand, for an Arab audience, signs of ebullience and energy in both content and delivery add to a speaker's credibility.

Age. There are also major cultural variances in the perception of age. Looking at an American fashion magazine or TV program clearly demonstrates that American culture favors youth over old age. But, this condition does not exist in all cultures. In the Arab culture, for example, children kiss the hands of older people and respect their views and opinions. The same view is held in most Asian cultures. Both the Japanese and Chinese show great respect and value for older people, as do Filipinos and American Indians. An awareness of this cultural difference might prevent a speaker from using phrases that tend to belittle the elderly, such as telling an audience that more "youthful ideas" are needed to correct a problem.

At this point, a cautionary note is in order. You must always be careful in generalizing about foreign nationals who reside in the United States or members of co-cultural minority groups. Varying degrees of assimilation into the Euro-American culture will influence their world view. Some will still observe the traditions of their homeland, while others will have adopted the ways of their new home. The more heterogeneous a group is, the more difficult it is for a speaker to make reliable generalizations about the viewpoints and probable reactions of the audience.

Religious Characteristics

Religious orientations, much like culture, have a strong influence on how people perceive and live in the world. For thousands of years people have turned to religion for guidance, whether the teachings are from the *Bible, Vedas, Koran, Torah, I Ching,* or *Analects.* Religion has historically provided the peoples of the world with advice and values on how they should live their lives. Therefore, knowing the religious views of the listeners is an essential part of any audience analysis. For instance, any discussion on nutrition must consider that some Hindus do not eat meat and that most Muslims and many Jews refrain from pork. A speaker needs to examine how religion is translated into an individual's value system. Knowing the ethical underpinnings of Karma would enable the speaker to discuss the consequences of a proposal as it applies to the notion of "good deeds." Knowledge of the Hindu view toward reincarnation would help in selecting effective arguments for a persuasive speech on cloning.

Religious affiliations can influence one's thinking on a variety of matters. Obviously, we all have values and attitudes that are, to a degree, grounded in religion. Quakers would likely oppose most types of violent activity and be in favor of human rights' initiatives.

Someone who is a devout Catholic would probably be in opposition to abortion and most types of birth control. Jews, for thousands of years, have valued education and would probably be more inclined than others to support a tax increase if the money were earmarked for colleges and universities. Mormons have a strong commitment to self-help and see the church as part of the family. They believe that these two institutions, church and family, not the government, should take care of individuals who encounter financial problems. Therefore, they would not be expected to be strong supporters of government funded welfare programs but would probably be more disposed to "faith-based" help initiatives.

Again, remember that generalizations, whether about culture or religion, are not always reliable. People are complex and are shaped by a variety of forces—religion being but one. Additionally, not all members of a religion hold similar beliefs. Personal experience should tell you that not every Catholic opposes abortion, nor does every Muslim follow the Five Pillars of Islam. In short, an audience analysis must include as many areas as possible.

Age-Level Characteristics

As individuals move through the stages of life, their concerns and interest often change. People's accumulated personal experiences bring about changes in values and attitudes. Many of these changes are unique to the individual, but some are also broadly characteristic of an entire age group. Knowing about those age changes and how they influence listeners should be a part of audience analysis.

Persuasive Issues. Numerous studies and opinion polls have demonstrated that age plays a role in how issues are viewed. This research has confirmed that older people are more inclined to become entrenched in their opinions and are harder to convince, while younger people are more open to persuasion. Growing older also tends to make one more conservative, as people become "set in their ways." Therefore, it is not surprising that many older people differ with the younger generations on subjects such as Social Security, defense spending, pornography, censorship, abortion, prayer in school, same-sex marriage, and living together before marriage.

Fund of Knowledge. The age of an audience will also help determine their fund of knowledge and subjects of interest. An older audience will know more about John Wayne, Frank Sinatra, "Captain

Kangaroo," the AARP (American Association for Retired Persons), "Watergate," "boat people," and the "War on Poverty" than a group of high school students will. Thus, when selecting examples, you'll need to consider the age of the audience. References to the programs or the people appearing on MTV will probably be confusing to older adults, who seldom watch that channel. On the other hand, examples that refer to "the folly of the Tet offensive" or analogies that recall "the long lines to purchase gasoline in 1973" would be baffling to most young people.

Use of Language. The age level of your audience can be an important consideration in determining the appropriate vocabulary for a speech. The meanings attributed to expressions such as "chill out," "cool cat," "awesome," "stoned," "the pits," and "wasted" are clearly related to age. While there can be many exceptions to any generalization about a given age group, the experiences and resultant attitudes of an older audience will generally differ from those of a younger audience.

Gender Characteristics

There is a growing awareness that gender plays a key role in how people perceive and interact in society. While men and women share many common experiences, goals, values, and the like, they are also different in many ways. For example, women tend to be more nurturing than men. These gender differences can have important implications for public speaking. Therefore, it is essential to know the gender composition of the audience: Will it consist of mostly one sex, or will it be equally divided?

Values. The audience's gender composition governs everything from the choice of a subject to the examples used in the speech. Although they grow up in the same country, the two sexes are commonly socialized in different ways. A person's gender motivates her or him, in both subtle and manifest ways, to behave according to certain cultural norms. For example, women place emphasis on traditional values regarding family and child care. Polls show that women often hold different attitudes than men on social issues such as homelessness, rape, poverty, unwed mothers, the death penalty, contraception, equal rights, affirmative action, and sexual harassment.

Stereotyping. Changes in the United States over the last 50 years have enabled women to share a wider range of experiences than previously and have made them more conscious of the problems inherent in the social perception and treatment of females. Today, most American women would be offended if a male speaker referred to them as "girls" or "honey." A speaker could also suffer a loss of credibility by portraying female roles in a demeaning light. To speak as if only men were governors, judges, engineers, or corporation heads while only women were daycare workers, nurses, elementary schoolteachers, or homemakers is an example of insensitivity that could lower a speaker's credibility. Also, humor that returns to old stereotypes characterizing women as vain or "empty headed" is insulting and must be avoided.

Occupations

Being a member of a particular occupational group usually means adopting, either consciously or unconsciously, many of the values associated with that profession. In many instances, audiences are made up of people from a variety of occupational backgrounds. Knowing those backgrounds enables a speaker to locate the points shared by the majority of the listeners. A persuasive presentation on environmental issues given to a group of corporate representatives from the lumber industry would have to be crafted very differently than one given to a Sierra Club meeting. Similarly, a speech on the excesses of executive pay would need to be structured differently for an audience of hourly employees than a corporation's board of directors.

Educational Levels

The educational level of a potential audience is another important consideration. In most instances, more education connotes more knowledge. Therefore, the audience's educational level might also influence how much they know about the topic. The type of education your audience has should also be considered. Someone with a Ph.D. in the sciences has a different pool of information than an individual with a doctorate in the humanities.

There is also a link between culture and education. For instance, compared to students in the United States, students in Korea, Japan, and Germany have the equivalent of almost three more years of education by the time they finish high school. Additionally, cultures often stress different subjects in their educational curriculum. In much of Europe, history, language, and literature are emphasized.

In Japan, China, and other Asian cultures, the focus is on science. In Mexico, education stresses folklore and the arts. Finding out what your audience knows, or does not know, needs to be a part of your audience analysis.

Geographical Considerations

Interests and attitudes—and what you know and do not know—are partly shaped by geographic circumstances. Where people were raised and where they live helps to mold their beliefs, values, and actions. Whether you live in an area by design or by chance, it will expose you to certain topics and deny you access to others. For instance, someone from a rural community in Wyoming may hold a different view of multiculturalism than a person from Southern California, who has lived his or her entire life surrounded by diversity. Knowing the geographical background of an audience can provide insight into how its members may be predisposed to certain topics.

Acquiring Information About Your Audience

By now, you are probably wondering how to gather information about a group of listeners. Two factors will influence your ability to conduct an audience analysis. First, the amount of time given to prepare the speech, whether one minute or several weeks, is often beyond your control. Second, the availability of data has an impact on efforts to obtain audience information. Sometimes, information about the audience might be readily available from several sources, but on other occasions, you might end up addressing complete strangers. When information is not accessible, you may have to simply rely on educated guesses, common sense, and speculation. For example, if you step in front of an audience composed almost entirely of senior citizens, you can assume they will probably not be aware of contemporary slang usage, and they may be harder to persuade than a younger audience. However, if you are fortunate enough to have time to research the audience, some of the following suggestions should prove helpful.

Before Speaking

Shared Affiliations. If you are affiliated with any of the same cultural, social, or professional groups as the audience, you can gather information directly. For instance, if you are talking to members of your class, you share a number of common experiences that can be called on. Being a member of a specific ethnic group also enables you to understand the backgrounds of an audience if the majority of listeners share the same cultural heritage.

Public Opinion Polls. Published opinion polls yield information about audiences' interests, beliefs, attitudes, values, needs, motives, and the like. Results of polls such as the Gallup Report, CBS, *New York Times*, Harris, CNN, *USA Today*, and Pew appear regularly on television and in newspapers and magazines. They offer information regarding specific groups' views on issues as diverse as inflation, welfare, race relations, military operations, capital punishment, federal spending, term limits on political offices, gun control, drug legalization, control of the border, and sex education. These polls are often categorized by specific characteristics such as education, race, gender, age, and the like. Internet links to the various polls can be found by doing a search for "public opinion polls" on Google or other search engines.

Interviews. Interviews can provide valuable information about listeners. If some of the audience members can be questioned directly, you can gain information about their views on various topics. People who may not be potential audience members but are familiar with the audience can also be a source of information.

While Speaking

The methods just described deal with acquiring information before the speech begins. However, there are instances when you can collect information about the audience during the actual speech. Being able to adapt to the speaking situation is an important skill that a good speaker must develop. To help acquire this capability, here are some ways of gathering and using information during a presentation.

Verbal Information. Asking questions during the speech is an easy way to conduct an *ad hoc* audience analysis. For example, the audience could be asked for a show of hands as a means of detecting their attitudes toward, or knowledge about, the speech topic. Questions requiring a verbal response could also be used. Whether through raised hands or verbal answers, the feedback allows you to tailor the presentaton to the audience.

Nonverbal Information. Experienced speakers also rely on subtle nonverbal feedback during the speech to help with their audience analysis. They interpret listeners' eye contact, facial expressions, head nods, restless movement, and the like as an indication of audience confusion, lack of understanding, anger, frustration, agreement, or some other emotion.

Audience Responses. Being sensitive to the audience's mood helps the experienced speaker make "on-the-spot" adjustments to the presentation. On these occasions, you might use some of the following techniques.

- Incorporating interesting examples and stories.

- Directly arousing the listless members of the audience.

- Altering the rate of delivery.

- Using more humor.

- Walking toward or among the audience.

- Pausing in a dramatic way.

- Personalizing the information.

- Changing the organizational sequence during the speech.

- Repeating key ideas.

As a concluding warning, you should beware of potential pitfalls associated with any audience analysis. Demographic generalizations can be misleading. People are complex and unique. We are all much more than what our gender, race, age, culture, ethnicity, profession, religion, education, and the like say about us. While a detailed audience analysis can be helpful, you must also remember that no single characteristic defines who and what a person is.

Appraising the Speaking Occasion

The circumstances surrounding the presentation also play a vital role in determining the outcome. As noted earlier, communication does not take place in a vacuum. The role and influence of (1) the occasion, (2) the setting, and (3) time constraints must be considered. Topic selection, language, one's attire, and overall demeanor are partially controlled by the occasion. The cultural composition of the audience can influence how the occasion should be perceived.

Type of Occasion

When considering the occasion of the speech, ask some of the following questions:

- Have the people gathered only to hear the speech, or do they meet regularly?
- What will the audience be doing before, during, and after I talk?
- Is it a spontaneous or organized gathering?
- Will the group observe any established traditions?
- Will the occasion be formal or informal?
- Will the occasion be a panel discussion or a "stand up" speech?
- Will the audience be permitted to respond?
- How many people will attend?
- Are there any rituals or protocols that I should know about?

Physical Setting

Analyzing the physical surroundings involves answering as many of the following questions as possible:

- Is the speech being delivered indoors or outside?
- What type of room will be used—large or small? In a television studio or before a "live" audience?
- Will there be a table or a podium?
- How effective are the acoustics of the room?
- Will there be noises or outside distractions that might disturb the audience?
- How close will I be to the audience?
- Will people be sitting in circles or in rows? Will they be standing?
- Will there be a public-address system? What type of microphone is available—fixed, portable, or wireless?
- Are power outlets and extension cords available for electronic projectors?

- What will the lighting arrangements be like if using visual aids?

- Will there be barriers that must be removed to allow people in wheelchairs access to the facility?

Answers to questions such as these will influence the way the talk is delivered. For example, if only a few people are in the audience and it is an informal gathering, your delivery can be more relaxed. Speaking in a small room calls for less vocal volume than if in a larger space with many people. Even gestures and movements have to be adjusted to the physical setting.

Time Constraints

What time of the day or night will the speech be delivered? Most people are more vigorous and energetic during the day than at night. Hence, consider whether the listeners will be tired or alert because of the time. In addition, part of analyzing the occasion means learning the presentation's time limit. Will the speech be assigned a specific time limit or be "open-ended"? In either case, questions concerning time should be dealt with long before beginning research or preparing an outline.

Culture and Occasion

The audience's culture can obviously influence the occasion and setting. For instance, people from cultures that are ritualistic and formal, such as the Japanese and Germans, perceive a business meeting presentation very differently than Americans do. The Germans will attempt to conduct a meeting presentation in a formal manner, whereas the American representatives will probably try to move to a more informal atmosphere. An awareness of cultural differences will help you make the necessary adjustments to delivery and content.

Chapter Summary

The process of adapting the objective of the speech to a particular group of people requires careful analysis of the audience, which will help the speaker make reasonable predictions about how the audience will respond to the presentation. Valuable insight into the audience's values, beliefs, attitudes, needs, wants, and desires can be gained from information about their cultural background, religious characteristics, age, gender, occupation, education, group affiliations, travel experiences, and special interests. Data on these topics can be obtained from sources such as published opinion polls, reference books, computer searches, and interviews. Useful information about the audience can also be gathered while the speech is being given. The speaker can use both verbal and nonverbal information to assess the audience's reaction to his or her presentation. An experienced speaker should also take time to analyze the speaking occasion. This investigation consists of questions related to the kind of occasion the speaker will be facing, what the physical surroundings will be, and what will precede and follow the speech. By implementing the material gathered through an analysis of the listeners and the setting, a speaker can effectively adapt her or his message to fit the audience.

Concepts and Questions

1. As applied to public speaking, what is meant by the terms "audience analysis" and "adaptation"?

2. What special factors should be taken into consideration when speaking to members of a culturally diverse audience?

3. In what ways can you use your audience analysis during a speech? Be specific.

4. What are some ways to gather information about a specific audience?

5. Why are cultural values an important area of consideration when conducting an audience analysis?

6. Explain how being aware of the audience's age or education level might be an important consideration when preparing and presenting your speech.

Activities and Exercises

1. Prepare a list of what you consider your most important personal values. Conduct an interview with someone from another culture, and ask that person to discuss what he or she deems important. Make a comparison of the two sets of values. How are they alike? How do they differ? How could this cause a problem during a speech?

2. What factors would need to be considered if you were going to give the same speech to the following audiences?

   a. A group of high school seniors.

   b. Members of the city council.

   c. Your classmates in your speech class.

   d. A group of senior citizens.

   e. A group of medical doctors.

   f. Members from a collectivist culture.

3. Visit three or four speaking locations that would make different demands on a speaker's adjustment. Write a short essay discussing how you would adapt to each of settings.

4. Attend two or three speech situations (formal business presentation, classroom lecture, church sermon, political rally, award banquet, etc.). Prepare a short essay that discusses your view on how each speaker adapted to his or her audience and occasion. ✦

Chapter 4

Supporting the Message

Finding and Using Evidence

E*vidence, proof, facts, support, verification, substantiation,* and *confirmation* are all terms that carry a similar meaning in the public speaking context. They refer to materials used to help prove and clarify the validity of an idea, a necessary part of effective presentations. This chapter will explain the various types of supporting material, how they can be used to accomplish a specific purpose, and where to locate evidence to support an oral presentation.

The Importance of Evidence

"Why," is a word young children learn very early in life and use with great regularity. The reason for its popularity is obvious—we often do not want to accept someone else's assertion at face value. We want reasons when people urge us to believe in one thing or another. And if those reasons are inconsistent with our existing beliefs and perceptions, we will tend to reject the idea or proposal. This need to have some proof or a clear explanation before believing something applies to most daily activities, but it is especially important in the public speaking arena. In a public address, mere assertions and unsupported statements are not sufficiently convincing, and listeners normally require greater explanation and proof. For instance, a speaker advocating that an affirmative action program be ended because the intended objectives had been achieved would be expected to provide sufficient data and explanation to support the claim. Evidence not only helps prove the speaker's assertions, it also makes a speech more interesting and can assist listeners in remembering the main points.

Forms of Verbal Support

Not all facts are used to support an assertion. Data are sometimes used to solicit and hold listeners' attention. Some points, however, are fundamental and essential to achieving the speaker's objectives. The essential points that help make a presentation's ideas understandable and believable are called **forms of support.** These forms are used to clarify or prove the speech's important and essential assertions. While we will discuss these forms as individual entities, in reality a speaker will seldom be able to prove a point with a single piece of evidence. Hence, the various forms of support sometimes overlap (e.g., a factual illustration might also contain statistics). This situation makes the content of a speech similar to a jigsaw puzzle—just as it takes many pieces to complete the picture, the various forms of support must fit together and work in combination.

Illustrations

The most fundamental and common form of support is an **illustration**, which is a narration of an incident that amplifies, proves, or clarifies the point under consideration. The speaker is saying to the audience, "Here is an example of what I mean." An illustration can also be thought of as a story that supports the point the speaker is trying to make. Illustrations generally take one of two forms: factual or hypothetical.

Factual Illustrations. A detailed, factual (i.e., true) illustration is a striking and vivid story that answers the questions of who, what, where, when, and how. More important, it points the audience in the direction of the speaker's main assertion. The knowledge that something actually occurred is a source of interest and persuasion. Notice how interest is stirred in the following story offered by a speaker who wants the audience to "see" the seriousness of domestic violence.

> Let me tell you about my roommate, Molly. One night when I returned home from work, I found Molly locked in our bathroom. Through the door I could hear her crying. I knocked on the door repeatedly and urged her to please open the door. Eventually she did open the door. At first

glance what I saw made me sick to my stomach. There was Molly—her face covered with ugly bruises and her entire body trembling out of control. She told me she had had an argument with her boyfriend. As the verbal confrontation intensified, her boyfriend grew angrier and angrier until he finally punched her in the face. But that was just the beginning. He continued to hit her until she collapsed. Molly told me this was not the first time her boyfriend had hit her. It seems that Molly, like many other women, was a victim of domestic violence.

Hypothetical Illustrations. The hypothetical illustration is a fictional example that allows the audience to see "what could or might be." Hypothetical illustrations are usually used to mentally depict the *possibility* of future events. In other words, what might happen if certain circumstances or actions were or were not to occur? The question "What would happen if you had to move to a country where you didn't know the language?" allows the speaker to place the audience in the center of a germane, hypothetical situation. Notice in the following hypothetical illustration how a speaker tries to persuade the audience that overcrowding at national parks is a serious problem.

> Imagine that you and some of your friends have just arrived at the edge of the South Rim of the Grand Canyon and are about to begin a hike that had been planned for months. However, the hike is slightly delayed by having to drive around looking for a place to park, much like in a shopping mall parking lot at Christmas. Finding a parking space takes over an hour and is a mile away from the trail head. After finally reaching the trail, you are once again astonished by the size of the crowd in front of you. The line seems to run on for miles. As you and your friends finally step off on the trail you are rendered speechless by what you see. And what you see are piles of trash along the hiking trail. From the shopping center-like parking lot, to the long delays on the trail, to the mounds of trash everywhere, you begin to realize that overcrowding is destroying the Grand Canyon. Today I am here to tell you that what is true of the Grand Canyon is not the exception but rather the rule when applied to our national parks.

Specific Instances

Similar to an illustration, a specific instance is an example that omits much of the detail contained in a factual illustration. Normally, specific instances are no longer than a sentence or two. For instance, a claim that academic dishonesty can lead to significant personal problems is strengthened by revealing that "Last semester, a classmate obtained a research paper from an online website and handed it in verbatim. When the instructor discovered the paper had been plagiarized, the student was given an F in the course and expelled from the university." Regardless of the length, specific instances add strength and understanding to an idea.

Statistics

It is best to view statistics as examples. They represent a numerical method for proving or describing something. With statistics, the speaker is not talking about one or two cases or instances, but rather is attempting to measure and define many occurrences quantitatively. Statistics are used to represent facts numerically; they are generalizations derived from comparisons of individual events. In public speaking, statistics help support or prove a claim by summarizing and simplifying facts relating to the presentation topic. For example, instead of talking about how AIDS has affected one person, a speaker can use statistics to examine how the disease has infected 25 percent of the population in some African nations, and that the problem is considered so serious that Bill Gates has donated over $150 million to help fight the disease on that continent.

It is often persuasive to string a series of statistics together. Notice the series of statistics in the following speech dealing with the Mexican banking system.

> According to a recent report in the *Dallas Morning News*, 80 percent of Mexico's population does not use banks, which are considered untrustworthy and charge very high transaction fees—accounting for 31 percent of the banks' revenues. Banco de Mexico estimates that loans to Mexican businesses and private citizens total less than 9 percent of the nation's GDP. This figure is about one-sixth of the U.S. level.

As a general rule, when using statistics you should always provide the source, as was done in the first sentence of the banking example. Also, refrain from presenting too many statistics at one time—doing so can confuse and bore the audience. If you must use a lot of statistics to support you claim, work them into the presentation's visual aids.

Testimony

Public speakers frequently incorporate the work of an **expert** into their presentations. An expert is someone who, as a result of training, experience, or background, is an authority on the presentation topic. Authoritative testimony from a widely recognized expert can be a compelling form of evidence. Testimony can be used to show that the speaker's point is corroborated by experts in the field. If you are trying to convince an audience that aspirin is beneficial in helping reduce heart attacks, you might quote testimony of the Surgeon General or information from an article in a leading medical journal. Because the audience may not be familiar with the person being cited as an expert, you should include the source's credentials as part of the evidence. For instance, in giving a presentation on the contrasting values of collectivistic and individualistic cultures, a speaker might introduce testimony in the following manner:

> Professor Stella-Ting Toomey, a widely published and internationally recognized intercultural communication scholar, has written that more than two-thirds of the world's population lives in cultures that reflect high levels of collectivistic values. (Ting-Toomey and Kurogi, 1998)

Analogy

Whether in everyday, casual conversation or on the public speaking platform, everyone relies on analogies to help explain or prove a point. In a speech, an **analogy** asks the audience to compare one idea or item to another. An analogy is used to suggest that item A "resembles," "is similar to," or "is not as good as" item B. Similarities are pointed out in regard to data, ideas, experiences, projects, institutions, or individuals, and conclusions are drawn on the basis of those similarities. Because analogies compare the unknown to the known, people can easily relate to them.

Analogies are usually divided into two types, figurative and literal. *Figurative analogies* compare things of different classes, such as the workings of a college library and the workings of the human circulatory system, not wearing a helmet when riding a motorcycle and SCUBA diving without oxygen tanks, or the theory of aerodynamics and the flight of birds. The *literal analogy* compares items, ideas, institutions, people, projects, data, or experiences of the same class, such as one automobile model to another, one political party to another, or one athletic team to another. The reasoning is that if two or more things of the same class contain identical or nearly identical characteristics, certain conclusions that are true in one case may also be true in the other. The similarity of the ideas being discussed gives the literal analogy its persuasive influence. If you believe and understand one, you should believe and understand the other because they are basically the same.

When using analogies, you must ensure they can be understood by a culturally diverse audience. For example, members of a culture that does not play basketball might struggle with the following analogy: "We all know that the taller the player, the easier the slam dunk. The same is true of a person trying to master a volleyball spike."

How to Test Evidence

An important criterion for using evidence in a speech is to ensure that it will be believed by the audience and that it is ethical. You can ask yourself several questions to help achieve these two objectives.

1. Is the specific evidence a typical case or an isolated enigma? Ensure that there are other pieces of evidence that corroborate the evidence being offered.

2. Does the support relate directly to the assertion being advanced? On too many occasions speakers offer support that might be interesting but that does not relate to the point being made. For example, a speaker wanting to prove that gasoline prices are too high, attempted to verify the statement by noting that the sale of riding horses in the United States has greatly increased during the last six months. Any audience would easily see that in today's society there is no connection between the price of gas and riding horses.

3. Is the evidence accurate? It is unethical and would greatly lower speaker credibility to use evidence that had been fabricated or distorted.

How to Use Evidence

Since evidence comes in many forms, a good speaker learns how to adapt her or his style to suit the supporting material. Learning how to effectively use the various types of supporting material takes practice and experience. There are, however, some commonly used techniques.

Direct Quotations or Paraphrases?

On some occasions, evidence should be presented as a **direct quote**. This is usually the case with statistics and expert testimony. In fact, speaker credibility is enhanced and the impact of the statistics or testimony is often greater when the material is presented in its original form. There will also be times when paraphrasing may be appropriate. In **paraphrasing**, the passage containing the evidence is restated in the speaker's own words. More than a summary, a paraphrase is a restatement of the original passage into a style more suited to the speaker, the audience, and the occasion. This can be particularly important when addressing a multicultural audience, because the need to paraphrase takes on added significance when English is the audience's second language. For instance, you may need to simplify complex material or explain a culturally specific example.

Transitions

Transitions, which can be words, phrases, or sentences, serve several functions. Primarily, they provide a speech with a smooth flow as the speaker moves from idea to idea and they make it easier for the audience to remember key points. When used with evidence, transitions show relationships between ideas and the evidence. Transitions tell listeners the speaker has completed one thought or piece of evidence and is about to move to something else. They lead the audience from one point to another. Transitions can take a variety of forms, including:

1. *Bridging.* Bridging informs the audience the speaker is moving from the current topic to the next topic. For instance, a speaker who has been discussing the various cultural challenges associated with the rising rate of immigrants and wants to introduce statistics to illustrate the claim might say, "Our community also has a problem dealing with cross cultural healthcare. Local hospital records indicate that 20 per-

cent of all emergency room patients were recent immigrants to the United States. They come from very different health-care systems and many have limited English skills."

2. *Signposting.* Signposting enables a speaker to review what has already been discussed and highlight what is to come. The following example illustrates the twin functions of sign-posting: "As I have demonstrated, underage drinking is the cause of numerous traffic deaths in our community each year. Now, I want to talk about how easy it is for high school students to purchase alcohol from local convenience stores. Then we can examine some solutions to this serious problem."

3. *Spotlighting.* Spotlighting serves two purposes. First, it tells the audience the speaker is moving to another idea or piece of evidence. Additionally, it signals that what is coming next is important. "If you remember only one thing from my pre-sentation, think about this," is an example of spotlighting.

4. *Nonverbal transitions.* Effective transitions can be nonverbal as well as verbal. Leaning forward, smiling, pausing, or moving in one direction or another tells the audience that a new idea or form of support is about to be introduced.

Culture and Evidence

The audience must also be considered when deciding when and how to use evidence. It should be no surprise that there are cultural variations regarding the selection of forms of support. Cultures such as the Latin, Arabic, and African favor illustrations and stories over "facts," while most Germans, Euro-Americans, and the British demand statistics and the advice of experts if they are to be per-suaded. There are even cultural differences as to who can be called an "expert." In one culture, it might be an elderly person; in another culture, it could be someone with impressive professional creden-tials; in yet another culture, it could be someone with a prestigious family name. A full audience analysis is needed before deciding on what evidence to cite and how it to use it.

Research: Finding and Using Supporting Evidence

After selecting a topic, determining the objective, completing the audience analysis, and deciding what evidence you will need, the next step is to begin **research**—locating materials that will help accomplish the main goal. The importance of starting research early cannot be over emphasized, because the quality of your support material will be directly proportional to the time spent in locating sources.

The most frustrating part of conducting research is getting started, and part of that frustration often comes from not having a clearly defined topic. A speaker can quickly become overwhelmed with data if the subject is too broad. Conversely, if a subject is too narrow, locating enough information may prove difficult. The research effort is made much easier by moving from a general category to a more specific topic within that subject.

Identifying and using credible sources is critical to conducting good research. This can be a challenge because many sources are devoted to promoting a self-serving perspective; *this is particularly relevant to Internet sites.* For example, information on the hazards of smoking distributed by the tobacco industry should be examined critically as to the independence and objectivity of the conclusions.

Locating Resources

Entry into the "Information Age" has greatly expanded the availability of support data, as well as the means of accessing that material. Successful public speakers quickly learn how to identify and retrieve credible evidence that will support the ideas contained in their presentations. To help you in your research efforts, we have included a brief discussion of some of the various sources consulted by effective speakers as part of their speech preparation.

Personal Experience

Personal knowledge is the natural starting point for gathering speech materials. Speakers often choose to talk about a particular topic because it has a personal attraction, and some of the best speeches draw on personal experience as a major source of information. However, it is unwise to rely solely on personal background for supporting information. Everyone has perceptual limitations that shape her or his personal view of reality. What you have

learned and can recall are subject to your individual likes and dislikes. Personal experiences are useful and often necessary but have
limited value when used to the exclusion of other sources.

Interviews

As a research tool, interviews have several strong points. By interviewing experts involved with the speech topic, you gain access
to the most current information on the subject. Interviews can also
stimulate interest when they are reported in the speech, because the
audience is eager to learn what the experts have said about the
topic. However, interviews require considerable forethought and
planning in order to yield useful and relevant information.

As with almost everything else, the interview process is not im-
mune to the influence of culture. When interviewing someone from
a different culture, keep the following points in mind.

1. *Differences in gaining access.* Even the method used to contact
   someone for an interview is affected by culture. Although
   most of us might feel it is highly appropriate to contact people by phone and ask to schedule an interview, this process
   is unacceptable in many Asian cultures. For these cultures,
   the interviewer often needs a formal introduction by a
   friend or associate of the interviewee. This introduction
   would be followed up by formal correspondence requesting
   the interview, providing some background on the interviewer and the topic, and allowing the interviewee to set the
   time and place.

2. *Differences in greeting behavior.* The initial greeting given the
   interviewee is another area of concern. People from Western
   Europe, Japan, and South America expect a somewhat formal greeting. For initial meetings with someone from a formal culture, first names should not be used and attempts to
   initiate "small talk" should be avoided. Try to let the interviewee establish the level of formality or informality.

3. *Differences in communication style.* Be aware of problems associated with language when interviewing someone from another culture. One concern is the manner in which questions
   are asked and answered. The dominant American culture
   uses language in a direct manner, while many Asian cul-

tures are indirect. Most Euro-Americans, for example, express agreement or disagreement easily and quickly. However, the Japanese and Chinese avoid using the word "no," because it is considered too harsh and direct. They prefer to use more indirect and equivocal language rather than offer a direct answer that might offend their communication partner. These conflicting attitudes toward directness can affect the entire interview.

Writing, Phoning, Faxing, and E-mailing

Information from people and organizations can also be obtained by writing, phoning, faxing, or e-mailing the individual or organization. Letters have been used for centuries to make contact with other people. The widespread use of the other three methods reflects our movement into the "Information Age." When using these means to correspond, start early and allow the recipient sufficient time to respond.

Organizations and Agencies. Countless organizations and agencies exist with the specific mission of gathering and disseminating information about certain topics. These organizations can represent commercial endeavors, healthcare issues, environmental concerns, or specialized interests. Most non-governmental organizations are listed in the *Encyclopedia of Associations*, a multi-volume reference book found in most libraries. This helpful guide is constantly updated and consists of several separate volumes that provide information on international, national, regional, state, and local organizations. Another library resource is *Associations Unlimited*, an online database containing background and contact information on associations, professional societies, and nonprofit organizations.

Government Agencies. Information from government agencies can be acquired by writing letters, making phone calls, faxing, or using the Internet. For example, comprehensive information on other nations is available from "Country Background Notes" at the U.S. State Department Internet site (<www.state.gov>), while the CIA's website (<www.cia.gov>) offers online access to the *World Fact Book*. U.S. demographic information can be obtained from the U.S. Census Bureau (<www.census.gov>), and the U.S. Department of Education (<www.edu.gov>) provides data on multicultural education.

Visual Electronic Media

Over the last 20 years, visual communication has become one of the fastest-growing industries in the world. Most colleges and universities now have media centers, where films, commercial and noncommercial videotapes, audiocassettes, CDs, and DVDs are available. Learning to use such resources can add a valuable dimension to your presentation. As an example, video clips from movies like *Jerry McGuire*, *Remember the Titans*, and *Barbershop* can provide the audience vivid illustrations of the difference between African-American and Euro-American communication styles.

Using the Library

Today, computers permit a great deal of research to be done from home. However, the library remains a wonderful place to gather material. To make your visits to the library more productive, this section examines (1) library reference sources, (2) electronic databases, and (3) traditional printed material in the library.

Library Reference Sources

Although similarities exist, no two libraries are alike. Learn about the following features at the library you will be using:

- The library catalog system.

- The interlibrary loan system.

- The location of indexes, abstracts, reference books, government documents, any special collections, and non-print media archives.

- Available electronic databases.

All major college and university libraries, and most public libraries, provide electronic catalogues of their holdings of professional journals, magazines, newspapers, books, and government reports. Learning to access these listings will be critical to the success of your entire college career. Since most libraries offer detailed tours of both the facilities and the procedures, consider taking one of these tours as part of your speech training.

Electronic Databases

Fast and easy-to-use computerized databases have become essential tools for conducting research. Some of the more popular databases for a broad range of topics are ProQuest Research Library, Educational Resources Information Center (ERIC), ABI/INFORM, Academic Search Premier (EBSCO), and LexisNexis Academic. Many other digital databases can be found listed under their general subject areas, such as Area and Cultural Studies, Business, Education, Language and Linguistics, Religious Studies, and Women's Studies. Since the list of available electronic databases is continually expanding and specializing, it is always worthwhile to request the assistance of a librarian knowledgeable about the various databases in your library. Of note, in addition to English, the ERIC database is available in Spanish, French, Japanese, Korean, and Chinese.

Library Printed Material

Although the following section focuses on the printed material available in the library, in many cases these same materials can be accessed electronically.

Reference Books. Researchers often begin their investigation by examining encyclopedias, which are easy to use, are usually kept up to date, and provide a broad overview of numerous topics. The most commonly used general encyclopedias are *Encyclopaedia Britannica* and *Encyclopedia Americana*. There are also a wide number of specialized encyclopedias and reference books that examine specific topics, such as education, social sciences, psychology, religion, art, government documents, science and technology, and famous individuals. Many of these sources are now available on CD-ROM, such as *Microsoft Encarta*. A reference librarian can always provide recommendations on the encyclopedias appropriate for your topic.

Magazines, Journals, and Pamphlets. There are hundreds of national and international magazines available to support research efforts. Some publications cover a wide range of subjects (e.g., *Time, Newsweek, The Economist*) and others focus more on specific topics (e.g., *Business Week, Forbes, Scientific American*), or specific regions (e.g., *Business Mexico, Far East Economic Review*).

In addition to the countless magazines written for the general public, thousands of specialized journals and trade magazines are produced for smaller, specific audiences. Whether the topic is advertising, broadcasting, health, recreation, public relations, world affairs, religion, law, psychology, education, political science, sociology, communication, engineering, academic or international trade, a wide selection of publications is available.

Atlases and Gazetteers. Because of growing international interdependencies, what happens in one part of the world often affects the entire planet. These dynamics necessitate knowledge of other cultures' locations and physical environments. Atlases and gazetteers provide this information. In addition to maps, atlases contain charts, tables, plates, and even statistical information about the regions, countries, and states. Gazetteers are actually a type of geographical dictionary that can help with location, spelling, and pronunciation.

Newspapers. Newspapers are an excellent source of information on current events and issues. Most influential newspapers can either be read via the Internet or found in the library. Several major U.S. newspapers are now indexed, making it much easier to locate specific information. Some of the leading newspapers that are indexed are the *New York Times, Wall Street Journal, Christian Science Monitor, Los Angeles Times,* and *Washington Post.* The indexes are usually held in the library reference room. When investigating a local or regional issue, it is also helpful to consult local newspapers. For an international perspective, the *London Times* and the *International Herald Tribune* are highly regarded English language foreign newspapers.

Because of the many U.S. ethnic populations, most libraries carry a number of newspapers from other countries, as well as papers designed for local ethnic populations. Some of these newspapers are printed entirely in English (e.g., *Japan Times, The Straits Times* from Singapore, *Cairo Times* from Egypt, or *The Santiago Times* from Chile) or have English supplements. When preparing a speech involving topics or people from another culture, it is often helpful to consult a newspaper that directly serves the people of that social group.

Government Publications. Most libraries have a special area that houses the thousands of reports, books, and pamphlets produced each year by local, state, and federal agencies. The library staff can show you where these sources are kept and how they are indexed.

Indexes. Indexes serve as a "finding aid" by providing an organized grouping of terms that help the researcher locate information on specific topics. Some examples are the *Biological and Agricultural Index, International Index, Art Index, Biography Index, Education Index, American Statistical Index, Index to International Statistics, Statistical Reference Index, Business Periodicals Index, Humanities Index, Public Affairs Information Index,* and *Social Sciences Index.* Because every library holds a variety of different materials, some of these indexes may not be available through your school's library. Additionally, some of the indexes have recently switched to digital formats and stopped publishing hardcopy volumes.

Microfilms, Microfiche, and Ultramicrofiche. Prior to the digitization of information, libraries used several different film formats to save space and facilitate access to printed materials. Collectively, these different types of film are known as microforms. Virtually all kinds of older printed material can be found on microfilm, microfiche, or ultramicrofiche. Each form uses a projection device for reading and copying. Assistance in the operation of these devices is available from the library staff working in the microform area.

Using the Internet

Although the Internet consists of many components, we are most concerned with accessing information, graphics, and audio from sites around the world. To help you appreciate the Internet as a tool for conducting research, we address four questions.

1. *What is the Internet?* In simple terms, the Internet is a global collection of computer networks that allows access to millions of pieces of information housed in computers all over the world. Information resources on the Internet closely replicate some of those found in the library and include such things as online journals, magazines, and newspapers; professional and governmental archives and databases; access to academic and public libraries; access to commercial databases and abstract services; and an endless supply of commercial, organizational, and private websites.

2. *How is the Internet used to find general information?* Search engines (e.g., Google and Yahoo!) provide the easiest and most efficient way to use the Internet as a research tool. Search engines catalogue thousands of subjects into various categories, which serve as a kind of table of contents.

3. *How do you narrow an Internet search?* The search engines usually produce a broad listing of sites relating to the requested topic. It is necessary to limit your search by using key words or phrases, especially at the beginning, to facilitate a more focused search. For example, research for a speech concerning the history of art during the Chinese Ming Dynasty (1368–1644) should avoid general terms like "China" and "art" and instead be more specific and use the phrase "Ming Dynasty art." Because not all search programs use the same databases, check more than one search engine when using key words or phrases.

4. *What precautions should be taken when using Internet material?* A common misperception is that if something is on the Internet, it is both true and reliable. This is patently false. Not only does the Internet contain superfluous and inaccurate data, in some instances the information is designed to intentionally mislead. For example, some people have actually driven to Mankato, Minnesota, in hopes of viewing whales on the Minnesota River after visiting a web site reporting their existence (Kelly, 1999).

Anyone conducting research on the Internet must critically analyze the material to separate valid and objective data from what is biased or fallacious. A series of questions designed to help students evaluate Internet websites has been prepared by Ithaca College and are available at: <http://www.ithaca.edu/looksharp/resources_factfiction.php#criteria>.

Citing Research Material

A problem that commonly plagues public speaking students is the proper citing of reference materials, particularly in speech outlines. Although there are numerous methods of citing research data, two of the most popular bibliographic formats are those from the Modern Language Association (MLA) and the American Psychological Association (APA). Both organizations publish style manuals that provide instructions and examples for citing almost all types of support material.

Ethics in Research

The ethical implications associated with conducting research and reporting findings are a particularly important topic. Within the last few years, several journalists have been discovered using bogus information in their reporting and have ultimately lost their jobs. Researchers who are discovered passing off others' data as their own are quickly discredited and saddled with a stigma that can never be erased. Authors who failed to properly cite borrowed material have been sued in court. To help you avoid these pitfalls, this section offers advice on to how to be an ethically responsible researcher.

Evaluating Sources

Too often, speakers consult only materials that are easy to locate or that support preconceived ideas. In these instances, the speaker may not obtain an accurate and balanced examination of the question being investigated. To be ethical, a speaker must strive to eliminate biases by examining material on both sides of an issue. For instance, a speaker researching the topic of providing state driver's licenses to illegal immigrants would want to collect information that presents arguments both for and against the measure. Additional questions that should be asked when evaluating a source include: Is the source current? Is the source credible? Does the source agree with findings from the other reference material, and if not, why?

Avoiding Plagiarism

Plagiarism occurs when a writer or speaker offers the exact or paraphrased words of someone else as if they were her or his own; it must always be avoided. Plagiarism is nothing more than a form of intellectual thievery, exactly like illegally copying music CDs or video DVDs. It is stealing from someone else. Remember, what is called plagiarism in college is considered copyright infringement in the corporate world, where it carries serious legal sanctions. To be ethical and to avoid even the slightest appearance of plagiarism, follow these guidelines when using research material:

- When using someone's exact words, give proper acknowledgment.

- When paraphrasing, tell the audience where the information came from.

Chapter Summary

An effective speaker understands how to use evidence to support and clarify assertions and observations. Evidence used in oral presentations can take the form of factual illustrations, hypothetical illustrations, specific instances, statistics, testimony, analogy, and visual support. An important consideration is how and when to use evidence. Techniques such as direct quotations, paraphrasing, and transitions are instrumental to effective public speaking, especially when addressing a multicultural audience. The most successful transitions take the form of bridging, signposting, spotlighting, nonverbal actions, and summarizing. Culture plays an important role in the use of evidence.

There are numerous resources for locating research material. Once the speech topic and objective have been determined, you can find information by examining your own personal experiences; conducting interviews; writing, telephoning, faxing, or e-mailing requests for material; investigating visual electronic media; using the library to consult reference books, magazines and pamphlets, academic journals, newspapers, subject indexes, and electronic databases; and searching the Internet. Determining the credibility and objectivity of source material is an important aspect in locating support material. The ethical considerations of conducting and presenting research material are a salient aspect of public speaking.

Concepts and Questions

1. Identify and explain three kinds of support/evidence.

2. What factors should be kept in mind when using statistics?

3. What is the difference between literal and figurative analogies?

4. What are effective transitional devices?

5. Why is the interview a good source of information?

6. Identify and describe three electronic databases that might be useful in conducting research.

7. What are some advantages and disadvantages of using the Internet as a research tool?

8. What are some ethical considerations to follow when conducting research?

Activities and Exercises

1. Write an assertion pertaining to a topic that is currently in the news. Then attempt to locate a factual illustration, two sets of statistics, and expert testimony to support that assertion.

2. Read a detailed story in a newsmagazine. Identify the various forms of support in the story.

3. Write a literal analogy on any subject you like. Then write a figurative analogy on the same topic.

4. Read a recent presidential "State of the Union" address. Analyze the speech for the forms of support used by the president. Ask yourself if the evidence supported the various points made by the president.

5. Visit the campus library and make a list of the various locations for all the research sources discussed in this chapter.

6. Go online and try to locate information on any of the following topics:

   a. Problems associated with an increasing world population.

   b. Teenage drinking in England.

   c. Mexico's higher education system.

   d. Global warming and desertification.

References

Kelly, T. (1999). Whales in the Minnesota River. *New York Times*. Retrieved 21 March 2006. <http://descy.50megs.com/mankato/NYT/nyt34.html>.

Ting-Toomey, S., & Kurogi, A. (1998). Facework competence in intercultural conflict: An updated face-negotiation theory. *International Journal of Intercultural Relations*, 22(2): 187–225. ✦

Chapter 5

Organizing the Message

Being Clear and Understandable

You have no doubt experienced a communication interaction, be it a casual conversation, a group discussion, or a public presentation, with someone who was disorganized. Perhaps the person tended to leap from one point to another, or maybe he or she seemed to ramble without a clear objective, or kept interjecting extraneous information. In these instances, the result was that you quickly lost interest in what was being said because the speaker was unorganized. On the other hand, the benefits from well-structured ideas and materials are numerous. For the public speaker, there are four major advantages to being organized:

The Importance of Organization

1. The organizational process identifies where additional evidence is needed to support a point or where logical flaws might be present.

2. A clear organization helps the audience understand and retain the presentation's primary points.

3. Material organized into a meaningful sequence highlights the relationship between the primary and subordinate ideas.

4. When a presentation is well organized, the audience will assign greater credibility to both the information and the speaker.

In short, a well-planned and ordered presentation helps listeners remain attentive and promotes greater understanding.

There are a variety of ways to organize a speech, but we will concentrate on the method that involves (1) formulating a core statement that expresses the presentations' central idea, (2) preparing main points and subpoints to support the core statement, and (3) choosing appropriate patterns to show how the main points relate to one another. These elements of speech organization are based on the assumption that the presentation will be divided into three major parts: introduction, body, and conclusion.

Core Statement

When you are starting to assemble materials for a presentation, it is important to keep in mind both the general purpose (i.e., to persuade, inform, or entertain) and the specific objective of the speech. To do so, you need to construct a single-sentence **core statement**, which serves as the unifying element for assembling the materials that help accomplish the general and specific purposes. It is a focused declaration of what the speech is expected to accomplish. For example, if you believe that people waste their money by not purchasing generic drugs your core statement might be "Whenever possible you should buy generic drugs." This core statement has one central idea, is worded in specific language, is a complete sentence, and centers on the audience.

Informative Core Statements

If the general purpose is to inform and the specific purpose is "to have the audience understand the important aspects to consider when buying a new car," the core statement might be "The principal features to look for when buying a new car are price, fuel efficiency, manufacture's warranty, projected maintenance costs, and insurance premiums." This core statement suggests the way supporting materials can be organized into orderly groups.

The core statement of an informative speech might delineate the steps in a process, the individual parts of a whole, or the characteristics that distinguish the topic from related subjects. For example, "Wine making involves pressing, filtration, fermentation, bottling, and aging" demonstrates a process, while "Stage fright is a form of communication apprehension specific to a given communication encounter" specifies stage fright as a subset of communication apprehension in general.

Persuasive Core Statements

If the speech is designed to persuade, the core statement might be phrased as a declaration of policy, such as "Off-shore oil drilling should be prohibited along the Southern California coastline." Alternatively, it might be worded as a value judgment, such as "Air travel is safer than auto travel." It can also take the form of a statement alleging something to be true, such as "Industrial pollution is the principal cause of global warming."

Ideally, the core statement should be prepared as soon as the research material has been gathered and analyzed. In wording the core statement, be careful to phrase it in terms broad enough to cover all the major areas included in the speech yet specific enough to provide a general idea of what will not be covered. Compare the phrasing of the following two core statements:

Core Statement A: Successful weight loss involves several considerations.

Core Statement B: Successful weight loss involves a proper diet, proper exercise, and a positive mental attitude.

Statement A suffers from the ambiguity of "several considerations," while Statement B indicates precisely what will be discussed.

Composing a core statement at the start of the organizing process provides a means of determining the relevance of the material to be used for the speech. Any proposed main point, subpoint, or item of supporting data that does not relate to the core statement is irrelevant and can be discarded. This process helps ensure the continuity of the speech.

Preparing Main Points and Subpoints

The next step is to decide on the main points that will clarify, reinforce, or prove the core statement. It is more important to plan the body of the speech before moving to the introduction and conclusion, because the main points will serve as the principal units of the body. Hence, begin the organizational process by translating the core statement into main points and subpoints. Most speeches have two to five main points. Like the core statement, the main points are also worded as statements, but each point deals with only one aspect of the core statement. For example:

Core Statement: The key factors in selecting a room air conditioner are ease of installation, cooling efficiency, and energy consumption.

> **Main Point:** I. Ease of installation depends on the size of the window opening, the weight of the cabinet, and the type of mounting hardware.

> **Main Point:** II. Cooling efficiency is dependent on the unit's BTU rating, the thermostat, and the size and condition of the room to be cooled.

> **Main Point:** III. Energy consumption is directly related to the size of the motor.

When selecting and phrasing the main points of a speech, (1) make certain each main points has a direct relationship to the core statement, (2) ensure that each main point is clearly distinguishable (separated) from the other main points, and (3) be sure that the main points, taken collectively, develop the core statement completely. These three important ideas require a more detailed explanation.

Relationship to the Core Statement

A main point statement must contribute directly to the proof, explanation, or illustration of the core statement. One way to determine whether a statement is a main point in a persuasive speech is to place connectives such as *because* and *for* between the core statement and the main point in question. The following is an example:

Core Statement: You should buy term life insurance, *because*

I.   It provides sufficient coverage at less cost than whole-life.

II. It is convertible to whole-life.

III. It is usually renewable.

The relationship between the core statement and the main points of an informative speech may be checked by using such phrases as *namely, for example,* and *in that.*

Core Statement: Green tea has attractive features, *namely,*

I.   It is inexpensive.

II. It is widely available.

III. It is low in caffeine.

IV. It has health benefits.

Separation From Other Main Points

Although the main points have a common kinship to the core statement, they should nonetheless *be separate from one another.*

Core Statement: You should buy generic drugs.

I.   They are just as effective as brand-name drugs.

II. They are cheaper than brand-name drugs.

III. They are often more readily available than brand-name drugs.

IV. They are as safe as the brand name drugs.

Organizational Patterns

The organizational pattern of a public speech plays an important role in audience reception and understanding, because people develop habits of organizing perceptions into meaningful contexts. Some things are perceived within a time frame, others from the perspective of their spatial arrangement, and still others in terms of logical parts, components, or divisions. Since the list of possible organizational patterns is lengthy, we will concentrate on those that have proven particularly effective for public speakers.

Chronological Pattern

Many subjects can be developed in a chronological (time) sequence. Chronologically arranged presentations usually begin with the early development of the subject and work forward to the present. Most obvious are speeches that deal with the steps in a logical progression—speeches that examine historical matters or presentations on how to do or make something. For example, a speech on events leading to the war in Iraq or a presentation about the different steps in making tofu could be organized chronologically. The chronological pattern is also effective when examining a person's life. Notice the time sequence in the following example:

I.   The life of Martin Luther King, Jr., clearly reflects the many influences of his nonviolent philosophy.

  A. The influence of his family.

    B. The influence of his early education.

    C. The influence of his meeting with Mahatma Gandhi.

A chronological pattern is also used when providing instructions or describing a process. The following example illustrates how the time pattern applies to a speech describing the manufacture of tofu:

Core Statement: The manufacturing of tofu involves four basic procedures.

I. Soymilk is prepared and heated.

II. Coagulant (e.g., calcium sulfate) is added to the heated soymilk.

III. The coagulated material is drained and transferred to a tofu mold.

IV. The tofu is removed from the mold and submerged in cold water for one hour.

It is easy to overwhelm listeners with a large amount of data, so when using a chronological pattern limit the number of main points to no more than three to five. Doing so helps the audience to understand and retain the information.

Spatial Pattern

As the name implies, spatial patterns organize main points around how various parts connect to each other. Geographical topics fit neatly into this pattern. For example, if talking about the potential for global overpopulation, population growth in the various world regions could be discussed.

Core Statement: The increase in the world's population is a serious problem.

I. Population growth in Africa.

II. Population growth in Asia.

III. Population growth in the Middle East.

IV. Population growth in Latin America and South America.

Speeches about the growth of an empire, the spread of a disease, or the location of natural resources are all examples of how one might use a spatial pattern with a geographical topic. If the subject is suitable, a spatial pattern can also be combined with a chronological pattern:

> **Core Statement:** During the last hundred years museums devoted to children have opened in a number of locations throughout the United States.
>
> I.   The Brooklyn Children's Museum was founded in 1899.
>
> II. The Children's Museum of Boston was founded in 1913.
>
> III. The Eugene Field House and Toy Museum in St. Louis was founded in 1936.
>
> IV. The Exploratorium in the Palace of Fine Arts in San Francisco was founded in 1969.
>
> V.   The Please Touch Museum in Philadelphia was founded in 1976.
>
> VI. The Interactive Space Museum was opened in Washington, D.C., in 1996.

Spatial patterns often go from left to right, top to bottom, bottom to top, or front to back. They can also move in a descending order of importance. For instance, if the topic is preparing a home for an earthquake, divide the house into the sections that are most dangerous ("the garage area because of oil and gasoline") and those that are least dangerous ("make sure there will be enough food in the pantry").

Topical Pattern

Topical patterns are among the most widely used sequences in speech making. They are a particularly effective way of *calling attention to natural divisions and categories of a subject.* This approach suggests a classification or relationship exists among the different parts of the subject. The classification can relate to such things as roles, functions, component parts, qualities, features, and levels of hierarchy. Some examples will illustrate the wide array of speech topics that can be treated topically:

Core Statement: We send nonverbal messages with many parts of our body.

I.   Our eyes send messages.

II. The way we move sends messages.

III. Our facial expressions send messages.

IV. Our posture sends messages.

V.   What we wear sends messages.

Core Statement: The Chula Vista Community Plan is environmentally sound.

I.   The plan protects the lakes from runoff pollution.

II. The plan protects the wildlife.

III. The plan protects endangered plants.

Patterns of topical time and space relationships are especially useful for presenting purely illustrative material, such as in speeches of exhibition and description. It is also possible to combine a variety of these patterns within the same speech. The main points, for example, might follow a spatial pattern; the subheads developing a main point might use a topical pattern; and the subheads developing still another main point might use the chronological pattern.

The topical pattern must be used with care. Students often make the mistake of calling anything a "topic" and end up trying to combine unrelated items. An example of erroneously related topics is to discuss solutions to sleep disorders by examining prescription drugs, herbs, and the history of sleep disorders. Remember, regardless of the pattern selected, the link between major and minor topics must be obvious to the audience.

Cause-Effect Pattern

The cause-effect pattern organizes the content of the speech around a set of conditions seen as the cause of an event or a phenomenon. This organizational sequence describes why a particular "thing" occurred (causes) and what were the results [effects]. Notice in the following arrangement the main point (the cause) produced certain consequences [effects]:

Core Statement: The reduction of state funds for higher education (cause) has created serious problems.

I. The number of students being admitted to community colleges and state universities has been reduced. [effect]

II. Fewer classes are being offered. [effect]

III. The student-instructor ratio has been increased for classes. [effect]

IV. Tuition and student fees have been raised. [effect]

Problem-Solution Pattern

The problem-solution pattern is often seen as a longer and more elaborate version of the causal pattern. Many persuasive speeches lend themselves to the problem-solution pattern because of its simplicity. By convincing the audience that there is something wrong with the status quo (too many cell phones going off during class), they will be receptive to your solution (having cell phones turned off at the beginning of class). In these situations, the speaker is urging the adoption of a new policy or plan. It involves (1) presenting a problem area, (2) proposing a solution to the problem, and (3) defending the proposed solution. A problem-solution outline for graffiti control might take the following form:

Core Statement: The sale of spray paint to minors should be prohibited by law.

Problem:

I. Some minors use spray paint destructively.

A. They deface public buildings.

B. They deface private residences.

C. They deface pavement and sidewalks.

Solution:

II. A ban on sales of spray paint to minors would address this problem.

A. It would make access to spray paint much more difficult for minors.

    B. It would make minors more fully aware of community feeling about defacement of property.

Defense:

III. Such a ban is feasible.

    A. It is legally feasible.

    B. It is administratively feasible.

Defense:

IV. The disadvantages of a ban are minor.

    A. Stores selling spray paint would experience little decline in sales.

    B. Minors needing spray paint for legitimate use could obtain it through their parents.

Defense:

V. Banning sales to minors is the best solution.

    A. It is less costly than surveillance systems.

    B. It is a better deterrent than the threat of harsh punishment.

Notice that both the main heading and subheadings are topical groupings. The main headings involve the topics of problem, solution, and defense of solution. The subheadings are groupings of such topics as defacement, accessibility, awareness, and legal and administrative feasibility. The problem-solution pattern can take several forms. Obviously, the number of problems isolated and the solutions proposed will depend on the complexity of the problem and the amount of time available for the speech.

Motivated Sequence

For over fifty years, Professor Alan H. Monroe's *motivated sequence* has been a popular method of organizing speeches. This method entails five steps: (1) the *attention step,* in which the speaker secures initial audience attention; (2) the *need step,* in which the audience is made aware of the existence of a problem; (3) the *satisfaction step,* in which a solution to that problem is explained and defended; (4) the *visualization step,* in which the speaker envisions what the future will be like if the recommended solution is (or is not) put into practice; and (5) the *action step*, in which the audience is given directions for implementing the solution. Note the similarity between the problem-solution sequence and the need and satisfaction steps of the motivated sequence.

Professor Monroe indicated that when this sequence is applied to informational speeches, the *visualization* and *action* steps can be omitted. The *attention* step serves the same function as in a persuasive speech, while the *need* step is aimed at making the audience feel a need to know the information about to be presented. The *satisfaction* step would, of course, provide the needed information. Because the motivated sequence is such an effective organizational scheme, it is explained in much greater detail in the chapters on the informative speech and speeches to persuade.

Organizational Patterns and Culture

The organizational patterns we've discussed are most effective if the audience is composed primarily of members from the dominant U.S. culture. Euro-American cultural experiences have taught us to string ideas together in a manner that, while familiar to us, is not universal. Three examples will help clarify this idea. First, in the United States a deductive organizational pattern is common because it is highly structured—a characteristic admired in our culture. We often introduce broad categories, then move to specifics to explain the assertions. But not all cultures use this pattern. Second, because the Euro-American culture normally looks for causes behind events, the cause-effect pattern is a popular method of organizing. This pattern assumes there are reasons (causes) for all actions. Again, this is not the approach taken in many other cultures. Third, as previously discussed, much of the thinking in the Western world is linear—direct and straightforward. When we organize our thoughts, prose, or speeches, the connection between each point is clear and easy to see. But, as with so many other things, this form of organization is not used by all cultures.

It would be easy to assume that everyone in the world organizes their thoughts in the same manner, but this is simply not the case. A person's reasoning processes and ways of organizing ideas are products of their culture. In Northeast Asian cultures, the main point is often not clearly specified but rather embedded in a story, illustration, or parable. Also, some cultures, such as Asians and American Indians, use configural logic instead of linear methods. In configural schemes, the association between each point is not distinct or explicit. This type of pattern assumes that the listeners will make the connection on their own. Gaining information on the cultural background of the audience will aid in selecting the most appropriate organizational pattern. We do not suggest an abandonment of the Western organizational patterns, but rather that you be aware that those models are not used by everyone.

Outlining the Message

Although preparing a speech outline is often misunderstood and even dreaded by students, doing so is quite important because it is at this stage that the pieces begin to fit together. A common misconception is that outlining is something to do after the speech has been composed—an unnecessary requirement that instructors impose on students. In reality, outlines are an invaluable tool for ensuring that speeches are organized in a clear, unified manner.

Importance of Outlining

An **outline** is essentially a visual representation of the cognitive process used to put a speech together. Constructing a detailed outline offers a number of advantages. First, it shows the existence of any informational gaps, faulty reasoning, or areas where illustrations are needed. Second, a good outline demonstrates the interrelationships of the parts of the message, their proportions, the adequacy of their development, and how well they function as a whole. Finally, an outline serves as the first step in the process of preparing the notes used to deliver a talk.

Although experienced speakers may use an abbreviated outline consisting of only key words or phrases, beginning speakers profit more from using a complete-sentence outline. For persuasive speeches, it is especially important to use the complete-sentence outline form because logical relationships cannot be clearly expressed through the use of key words or phrases. Moreover, the extra effort required to construct a complete-sentence outline helps one to more easily remember ideas when actually giving the presentation.

Characteristics of Effective Outlines

It is difficult to say just how much of the actual speech should appear in the outline. The variables affecting this decision range from the degree of speaker familiarity with the topic to the amount of time allotted. However, as a general rule, the total number of words in an outline should equal no more than one-third to one-half of the words used during the talk. Regardless of the formula used, adhering to the following seven principles will assist you in preparing an outline:

1. *Assign only one idea or statement to each unit of the outline.* Doing so ensures the material is clear and free from auxiliary points. Notice in the following two illustrations how Example B is much more explicit than Example A.

Example A (Incorrect)

I.   Because it is cleaner and cheaper, solar power is preferable to fossil-fuel power; moreover, it has unlimited availability.

Example B (Correct)

I.   Solar power is preferable to fossil-fuel power, because

    A.   It is cleaner.

    B.   It is cheaper.

    C.   It has unlimited availability.

2. *Do not allow points to overlap.* The following example represents a violation of this rule:

I.   Large populations of Hispanics are found in all regions of the United States.

    A.   They are found in the East.

    B.   They are found in the West.

    C.   They are found in the North.

    D.   They are found in the South.

    E.   They are particularly numerous in California.

The inclusion of E throws the pattern into confusion, because a single state is not equivalent to a region.

3. *Maintain consistent levels of importance among coordinate points.* Units labeled as main points should share common elements. The inclusion of a unit of greater or lesser magnitude will disrupt the consistency of the pattern. For instance:

I. The Atkins diet has increased the consumption of meat in the United States.

    A. Sales of beef are up.

    B. Sales of pork are up.

    C. Sales of lamb are up.

    D. Sales of chicken are up.

    E. Sales of fish have decreased.

The inclusion of E breaks the consistency of the pattern and introduces a potentially confusing element of disproportion.

4. *Maintain clear levels of subordination.* The hierarchical relation of points is indicated by proper use of symbols and indentation. Compare Examples A and B that follow:

Example A

I. Cultures are formed and influenced by several factors.

    A. Geographical and environmental setting

    B. Economic considerations

    C. Socio-historical experience

    D. Evolving values

        1. Money or status

        2. Increased profits or more employment

        3. Individual privacy or social continuity

Example B

I. Cultures are formed and influenced by several factors.

    A. Geographical and environmental setting

    B. Economic considerations

    C. Socio-historical experience

II. Evolving Values

    A. Money or status

    B. Increased profits or more employment

    C. Individual privacy or social continuity

Notice that in Example B, Roman numeral II should not be a main point but rather should be part of the subordination to Roman numeral I.

5. *Use a consistent set of symbols and indentations to indicate relationships among main headings and subheadings.* The usual system is:

I. Main heading _____

    A. Subheading _____

        1. _____

           a. _____

               (1) _____

               (2) _____

           b. _____

        2. _____

    B. _____

II. _____

Note that main headings are consistently designated by Roman numerals; subheadings that explain, illustrate, or prove the main headings to which they are immediately subordinated are designated by capital letters; the level that is subordinate to the subheadings is designated by Arabic numerals; and so on down the scale of importance.

6. *Whenever possible, supporting points should be worded in parallel sentence form.* By using corresponding structure and language, the logic of the material is tested and made clear to the audience. Notice how Example B is much clearer than Example A in that each point in B begins with a common and consistent vocabulary:

Example A

I. Vitamins in your diet might be essential to good health.

    A. Some people say that niacin might be a possible cancer inhibitor.

    B. It has been suggested that folic acid may help protect against heart disease.

    C. It could be that vitamin D is related to some kidney diseases.

Example B

I. Vitamins in your diet might be essential to good health.

    A. Niacin may inhibit certain kinds of cancer.

    B. Folic acid may help protect against heart attack.

    C . Vitamin D may help prevent certain kidney diseases.

7. *An outline should have an introduction, body, and conclusion.*
Collectively, these three sections help the speaker visualize how all the parts of the speech fit together.

Introduction

I. Be careful the next time you approach that cute little boy playing with a toy gun—it may not be a toy.

Body

II. Juvenile crime is on the increase.

    A. Murder is on the increase among juveniles.

        1. Evidence

        2. Evidence

    B. Armed robbery is on the increase among juveniles.

        1. Evidence

        2. Evidence

    C. Aggravated assault is on the increase among juveniles.

        1. Evidence

2. Evidence

Conclusion

III. Juvenile crime is on the increase.

Using Transitions

You will recall that transitions are words, phrases, and sentences that connect your ideas to one another. Their major function is to tell listeners what has been done ("The statistics we have just looked at clearly demonstrate the widespread nature of this problem") and what is next ("Let us see if the experts agree with the data I have just presented").

As noted earlier, a transition can take a number of specific forms. Four of the more common ones are the (1) preview ("Now would be a good time for me to talk about the reasons our college does not have a suitable student health plan"), (2) summary ("Having looked at the major funding programs on campus, you can see why we do not have a suitable student health plan"), (3) summary-preview ("We now know what is wrong with the student health plan, but what can we do about it?"), and (4) numeration ("There are three reasons our health plan is not working. First, . . .").

As a general rule, transitions are not incorporated into the same system of symbolization and indentation that are part of a normal outline. They are usually shown in the following manner:

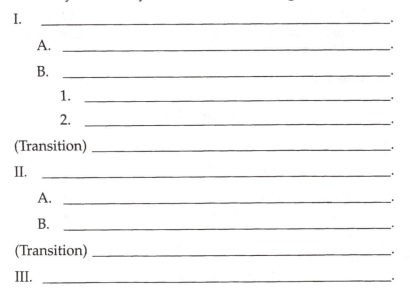

I. _____.

   A. _____.

   B. _____.

      1. _____.

      2. _____.

(Transition) _____.

II. _____.

   A. _____.

   B. _____.

(Transition) _____.

III. _____.

Chapter Summary

The process of assembling a speech usually begins with the construction of a core statement embodying the central idea of the speech. Growing out of the core statement are the main points, subpoints, and supporting materials. Main points should (1) relate to the core statement, (2) relate to one another yet be separable from one another, and (3) collectively develop the statement under which they stand. Material should be meaningfully organized around a logical sequence. The most common patterns of organizing are chronological, spatial, topical, cause-effect, problem-solution, and the motivated sequence.

An outline is a tool for arranging the parts of a message into an orderly sequence. A good outline features the use of a consistent set of symbols to show proper subordination of ideas. Each unit of the outline should contain only one idea; points should not be allowed to overlap; and coordinate points should be parallel.

Concepts and Questions

1. What are the benefits of good organization?

2. What are core statements, main points, and subpoints, and how are they related?

3. Differentiate among the various organizational approaches: chronological, spatial, topical, problem-solving, cause-effect, and the motivated sequence.

4. Why is it important for speakers to prepare outlines?

Activities and Exercises

1. As you listen to a speech in your class, try to outline the speaker's main points and subpoints.

2. Explain how you might use a chronological pattern when preparing a speech dealing with the Olympic Games.

3. Select any topic suited for a speech to inform. Explain how you would use any three of the patterns discussed in this chapter to outline the topic. ✦

Chapter 6

Displaying the Message

Visual Aids

Although they sometimes may sound cliché, there is considerable truth in the expressions, "Seeing is believing" and "A picture is worth a thousand words." The fact is that visual images designed to persuade, inform, or entertain can be powerful. This strength has been heightened by the proliferation of electronic media, which have greatly expanded our daily exposure to visual images. Because of the ever-increasing role of images in daily life, and because graphics can contribute markedly to the success, or failure, of your speech—we feel it is necessary to devote an entire chapter to the subject. Within the context of rhetoric and public speaking, visuals are commonly called **visual aids**, but are sometimes referred to as *graphics*.

Value of Visual Aids

Graphics have always been an important part of a public presentation, but their significance has been made even more salient by the increasing pervasiveness of visual media in the "Digital Age." As a result, today, more than ever before, audiences expect, and indeed need, public speakers to use visual aids to support their verbal messages.

The benefits derived from using graphics to support a public address cannot be over emphasized. They assist both the speaker and the audience. For example, a bar graph depicting a five year rise in the number of international terrorist events can help support an assertion that more funding is needed for border security. Some of the benefits of using visual aids in public address include:

- *Retention.* Visual aids can assist the audience with both memory and recall. When people see and hear a message, there is a much better chance that they will remember the point being made. By some estimates we retain only 20 percent of what we hear, yet when hearing is combined with seeing, the percentage jumps to nearly 50 percent.

- *Support.* Visual aids also serve as a means of support by making an idea concrete and persuasive. A picture of a classroom with students from various cultures has greater impact than simply citing statistics on multicultural education.

- *Clarity.* Graphics, such as a model, diagram, map, or picture, can help clarify complex material. Consider how the complex natural boundaries and national borders of the Middle East could be made less confusing by looking at a large map instead of hearing a speaker try to describe the territorial lines with only words.

- *Organization.* The structure and organizational sequence of a speech can be enhanced by visual aids. An overhead transparency or PowerPoint projection could display the major points of the speech or even help divide the presentation into its major parts.

- *Attention.* Visual aids also help capture and sustain audience attention by arousing and maintaining interest. A picture, an illustration, or a short list of key points provides listeners with a focal point.

- *Credibility.* Graphic support can also add to speaker credibility. Listeners are often impressed by the use and quality of visual aids, which signals the speaker's personal interest in the topic. Conversely, credibility may be diminished if the visual aids are poorly prepared or exhibited.

Culture and Visual Aids

Visual aids are particularly useful when speaking to people from other cultures, especially if English is their second language.

Seeing references to what is being talked about can help a multicultural audience better understand a difficult concept. For example, it might be easier for listeners from China to comprehend a speech on changes in U.S. fashions if they could see pictures of the clothes being discussed, instead of only hearing words such as "drape," "pleat," "inseam," and so on. Even being able to visually see some of the words in a speech might help nonnative speakers of English understand some of the concepts being discussed. There are also cultures (e.g., French, Japanese) whose members are cautious and deliberate in making decisions. They demand more background information and proof than Americans do. In these cases, the visual aid becomes another piece of evidence.

Considerations for Selecting Visual Aids

It is important to determine what type of visual aid is most appropriate for a presentation. With the rich variety of available graphic support, the speaker must choose carefully in order to match the occasion, the physical setting, and the audience. Each of the following considerations will influence visual aid selection.

- *Presentation objective.* Begin thinking about visual aids by asking, "What is the purpose of the presentation?" If the objective is to persuade, the supporting materials will likely be different than those for an informative speech. Choosing the most appropriate medium is usually a matter of common sense. Graphics providing detailed, in-depth statistics to illustrate the growing trade imbalance between developed and under- developed nations could be effective for a persuasive speech but might overwhelm an audience in a speech to inform.

- *Audience size.* Visual aids must be adapted to the size of the audience. Photographs, flip charts, and posters work well with a small group, where everyone is close to the speaker. However, overhead transparencies, document projectors, or other devices that can enlarge and project are necessary for large audiences.

- *Time, money, availability.* Issues such as time, money, and the availability of certain equipment also influence decisions about which aids to use. For example, color transparencies can be costly, and PowerPoint presentations require a computer and projector. The speaker has to select the medium that can produce the best visual aid using the available resources.

- *Expertise.* Well before the presentation, you must ensure you have the requisite knowledge for operating the visual aids. Doing so requires practicing with the actual graphics and audiovisual equipment that will be used during the speech. Speaker credibility can suffer from an inability to properly display the visual support materials.

Non-electronic Visual Aids

Contemporary information technologies have significantly expanded the selection of visual aid equipment available to speakers. However, there will be times when electronic aids may be inappropriate or simply unavailable. In those instances, you will have to resort to the more traditional aids. Therefore, a brief discussion of the various non-electronic means at your disposal is worthwhile.

People

You can add a visual dimension to a presentation by asking someone to serve as a visual aid. An individual can demonstrate the proper grip for holding a golf club, serve as a model for ethnic clothing, or demonstrate the correct way to perform a folkdance.

Objects

Reality is usually more compelling and attention holding than an abstract or a graphic representation. Objects allow listeners to see the item or process being discussed and greatly enhance the presentation. Examples include having a guide dog when describing programs to assist the disabled, a flower display when illustrating *ikebana* (Japanese flower arrangement), and different kinds of equipment when discussing first aid procedures.

Models

Models replicate the real thing and can serve three quite useful purposes. They can help explain a complex idea (e.g., the solar system), and they are easily moved from place to place (e.g., a model of the human skeleton). Also, the speaker can construct the model to focus on a specific aspect of the process or entity being discussed (e.g., the DNA helix to explain genetic engineering).

Posters

Posters can clarify and reinforce an idea or process. They are easy to construct, can be prepared ahead of time, can be tailored to meet specific needs, and require little effort. The only materials needed to make a simple poster are poster board and colored markers.

Maps

Maps are beneficial in helping the audience locate geographic points of reference. Suppose you wanted to explain the difficulties of securing Afghanistan's borders against terrorists and drug smugglers. A map displaying how Afghanistan is surrounded by Pakistan, China, Tajikistan, Uzbekistan, Turkmenistan, and Iran, would clearly illustrate the political complexities of the task. The Internet has increased the availability of maps and many can be downloaded for free (for instance, see the "Images" tab on the Google search engine).

Graphic Art

Paintings, drawings, sketches, cartoons, and photographs are helpful and readily available to speakers. You can make your own paintings or drawings, gather them from books and magazines, or use already prepared computer graphics packages from "clip art" files. Copy centers can enlarge almost any drawing or picture. If trying to explain the three different horizons contained in traditional Chinese scroll paintings, the task would be simplified by using an actual scroll painting or a photograph of one.

Charts and Graphs

Numbers or abstract, complicated ideas can often be made more comprehendible by using charts and graphs. A chart or a graph easily illustrates organizational hierarchies, statistics, and complex ideas. Think for a moment how much a bar or pie chart would improve a speech comparing the current United States ethnic population distribution with projections for the year 2050.

Chalkboards and Dry-Erase Boards

In this age of sophisticated technology, using a chalk or a dry-erase board might seem a rather mundane type of visual aid, but in some instances, nothing else may be available. Chalk or dry-erase boards are still common features in conference rooms, auditoriums, and classrooms. Additionally, a board allows a speaker to develop a step-by-step illustration of the process being explained. During the presentation, chalk or special pens can be used to add material that visually demonstrates how, for instance, a political campaign is planned and executed.

Flip Charts

Flip charts combine some characteristics of posters and chalkboards. The charts are usually large unlined tablets, secured to an easel, which can be written on with broad-tipped felt pens. They can also be used to display photos, maps, or other graphic material. Flip charts may be prepared in advance or developed during the presentation. Portable flip charts are helpful in rooms that have limited visual aid support. They are especially useful for speeches that explain a progression or process, such as the steps in wine making, because each page can be used to demonstrate a different stage of the procedure.

Handouts

Handouts should be provided when the information cannot be explained by using any other aid, when the audience needs time to carefully examine the material being discussed, or when the speaker wants the audience to retain a copy of the information. Handouts allow each member of the audience to have a copy of a long quotation, a diagram, a map, a chart, or an illustration. Many professional meetings and settings call for materials to be provided to the audience as part of the presentation (e.g., an organization's annual report).

Electronic Visual Aids

Technological advances have significantly eased the preparation of visual aids, and computers now make complex, multicolored graphics easy to produce and display. Businesses and industries are increasingly using computer-generated graphics to support presentations and training sessions. While we discuss various electronic visual aids here, our greatest emphasis will be on computer-generated graphics.

Slides

Just a few years ago, 35mm slides were considered top line visual aids, but with the development of digital photography, slides are now somewhat of a dinosaur for public speaking support. Since they are seldom used, we will simply indicate that much of the information discussed under digital photography can be applied to slides.

Transparencies

Although they have been used for decades and are not as dramatic as the new electronic technologies, transparencies remain one of the most popular and common visual aids. A **transparency** is a thin, clear sheet of plastic (acetate) bearing an image transferred from another document (magazine, newspaper, typed page, and so on). Transparencies are useful because they are simple to construct and easy to move from location to location. Using a felt-tip pen to write or draw on the plastic sheet, a speaker can quickly and easily stress any process, idea, or concept considered significant.

Transparencies are relatively inexpensive and can be made by anyone with access to a copy machine. The finished transparency is projected onto a screen by an overhead projector, commonly found in nearly every classroom or meeting room. In the event a screen is not available, the graphic can also be projected onto a blank, preferably white, wall. Transparencies can be made in advance or constructed during the speech. For example, using a map transparency, the speaker could trace the route of a forest fire while discussing the damage caused in the various affected areas.

As is the case with all the aids discussed in this chapter, transparencies must be used with care. If handled incorrectly, they can call attention to themselves, reduce your credibility, or lessen audience comprehension. Keep the following two ideas in mind when preparing and presenting transparencies. First, too much clutter and detail on a single transparency will only confuse the audience. If there is too much information for the audience to quickly and easily comprehend, they will have difficulty finding the focal point. Second, although it is a simple point, be sure that the projected image is level and upright on the screen. While it may give the audience a good laugh, the speaker can be very embarrassing to discover the graphic is reversed or upside down.

Electronic Displays

Electronic displays represent an important audiovisual tool that is growing in popularity, especially in light of their variety, flexibility, and portability. That almost all professional presentations are now done using electronic media attests to the importance of these graphics.

The various types of electronic displays include the older videotapes, the newer digital formats using CDs and DVDs, and computer based aids, such as PowerPoint. DVDs and computer-generated displays, both of which are compatible with digital video cameras, are rapidly displacing the older videotapes and CDs. These newer displays are normally used on computers connected to a data projector.

Videos used with these display systems can be either homemade or commercial productions. Most college campuses and large organizations have media centers that catalog, store, and circulate thousands of prerecorded graphics that are available for checkout. These graphics can be used to help clarify and explain various points of a speech.

The improved ability to easily interface digital cameras with computers represents one of the more modern and exciting phenomena in the communication field. The equipment for producing video "programs"is relatively inexpensive, lightweight, and simple to use. The portability of small digital cameras enables creative speakers to produce homemade videos and photos that are highly individualistic and unique. You could, for example, take a small video camera to a local *Cinco de Mayo* celebration and interview the participants for a speech dealing with Mexican-American customs. Pictures of people from various ethnic backgrounds engaged in communication encounters could provide visual aids to help demonstrate the cultural differences in nonverbal gestures.

Most data projectors are simple to start and stop, which permits the speaker to let the video do some of the "talking." With the aid of another person, a speaker can even be the "star"of her or his own production. The projectors also contain a number of features that can contribute to both interest and learning. Techniques such as replay, stop action, and slow motion afford an opportunity to stress particular parts of the graphic. Think of how effective it would be if, while talking about a folk dance of a particular culture, you were to show a video of someone dressed in traditional attire demonstrating the correct steps.

Computer Aids

Computer-Generated Graphics. Computer graphics have become an increasingly useful vehicle for producing presentation visual aids. They offer you a novel and effective means for visualizing material. The graphics are clear, readable, and interesting. Most home computers have the capability of producing line graphs, bar graphs, charts, and drawings, which can be printed in black and white or color. And, one does not have to be a computer genius to operate most of the programs. With the help of software programs such as PowerPoint or Freelance, you can design creative graphics or choose from hundreds of existing drawings. More advanced and complex graphics can be prepared using Photoshop or Illustrator software programs. When completed, the graphics can be displayed on the monitor, projected on a screen, or printed. Once on paper, computer-generated graphics can be turned into a transparency, made into a handout, or displayed as a traditional poster.

Word Processors. The many computer-based word processor programs provide an easy way to create visual aids. The software allows the creation of "bullet items" (short phrases) using a variety of typefaces that can be enhanced by bolding, shadowing, and line spacing. All these "tools" can make a visual aid informative and attractive, whether used as a transparency, poster, or handout.

When using computer aids, remember the following advice:

- Try to strike a balance between clarity and creativity. Because some graphics programs and laser printers allow for detailed and dazzling artwork, novices tend to over-do it. Try not to mix too many type styles or to add extra material simply because it is available. An overly stylized or complex graphic will distract the audience's attention away from what is being said.

- Always thoroughly proofread the graphics. Misspellings, word omissions, or obvious errors will detract from the presentation, reduce audience attention, and decrease speaker credibility.

- Allow ample time to produce the graphics so they can be incorporated into the practice sessions preceding the speech.

Audio Aids

Although this chapter is titled "Visual Aids," the role of audio in speech making must be briefly discussed. Audiotapes, CDs, DVDs, and digital recordings can make presentation material more interesting and memorable. A speech on the history and evolution of hip-hop would be enhanced by playing actual examples representing each musical period. A recording of Martin Luther King, Jr.'s "I Have a Dream" speech can make an indelible impression on an audience.

Multimedia Presentations

Multimedia presentations are becoming increasingly popular and commonplace. Stated simply, **multimedia** is the integration of two or more forms of visual/audio support. Expanding on the earlier example, the hip-hop speech could combine audio lyrics, a music video clip, still pictures, and text into a single PowerPoint presentation. While multimedia presentations can be very effective, beginning public speakers should approach them with caution. It takes considerable time to prepare a multimedia presentation and the potential for a technical malfunction during the speech is significantly increased.

Preparing Visual Aids

When preparing visual or audio aids, consider the following points:

- Conduct an audience analysis with your visual aids in mind. Ask yourself whether each visual aid is suited, in both content and form, for the audience and whether the aids help accomplish the objective of the presentation. Avoid using aids as "window dressing" in an attempt to make the speech more attractive.

- Be sure that the lettering, artwork, or other main features are large, clear, and of sufficient contrast for everyone in the audience to see. Try to use colors, contrasting shapes, and other techniques to keep the aids from appearing dull and ordinary. Reference sources are available that discuss the psychological effects of color, how color influences emotions, and considerations on the association between color and culture. *Using PowerPoint 2000*, published by QUE of Indianapolis, provides an overview of these considerations.

- Check the physical surroundings and furnishings before the presentation. Evaluate the location in advance to avoid discovering, after it is too late, that there is no place to put the chart or no electrical outlet easily available for electronic equipment. Notice barriers that might obstruct the audience's view (desks, podiums, etc.). Can the room be darkened? Where is the wall switch? Where is the electrical outlet? Will an extension cord be needed? Thinking about these sorts of issues will help avoid problems.

Using Visual Aids

The following guidelines can help promote effective use of visual aids.

- Remember to rehearse. Become familiar with all of the visual aids, the audiovisual equipment, and the room where the speech will be given.

- When using a television monitor, projection screen, or flip chart make sure that it is clearly visible to all audience members.

- Number the graphs so they can be maintained in the needed order before and during the speech.

- Ensure that the images—numbers, letters, pictures, or drawings—are large enough for everyone to see. Generally, a graphic should have no more than four or five words per line and only three to five lines of text.

- Display a visual aid only when it is being discussed. Blacken the screen or turn the projector "off" when not displaying an image. The bright light of the machine, or an image no longer being discussed, will become a major distraction to both the audience and yourself. Also, remember to turn off the machine once the last graphic has been shown.

- It is usually best to display only one visual aid at a time unless you are trying to demonstrate an interconnection between the two. Displaying two or more aids at a time can divide audience attention between the graphics and reduce their attentiveness.

- When an image is displayed, do not block the audience's view by stepping in front of it. Stand to the left or right of the graphic at an approximate 45-degree angle to the audience.

- When using a pointer, briefly pause, look at and place the pointer on the appropriate part of the image, then quickly turn back and begin addressing the audience. Remember to maintain eye contact with the audience. Do not become engrossed in the visual aid and forget the listeners. You want to talk *about* the graphic, not *to* the aid.

- When using your hand to point, gesture with the palm held toward the audience turned slightly upward. Always use the arm closest to the graphic; never reach across your body to point at the graphic.

- All electronic aids have the potential for mechanical problems, so be sure the equipment is in good working order and know how to operate it before beginning the speech. If something does malfunction during the presentation, try to handle the situation with wit and humor.

- Learn to anticipate and deal with the unexpected. Horror stories concerning the use of visual aids are legendary. Computers crashing, photographs sticking together, easels and tripods falling, colors running together because the graphic got wet while being transported, audiovisual equipment breaking during the talk, projector bulbs burning out, and "live" subjects upstaging the speaker are just a few of the problems that have beset presentations. Learn to have a contingency plan to help deal with the unexpected. Perhaps the best advice is to stay calm, keep going, and laugh at adversity. The audience will surely empathize with your situation.

Chapter Summary

Visual aids should be used whenever and wherever they will assist in accomplishing the speaker's objective. Visual aids let people "see" and can help make verbal messages more interesting, understandable, persuasive, and memorable, while adding to speaker credibility. In choosing the most appropriate aid, analyze the purpose of the talk, the size of the audience, the availability of certain aids, and personal expertise in using a particular aid. Explore the possibility of using a variety of visual aids, such as people, objects, specimens, models, posters, diagrams, maps, paintings, photographs, charts, graphs, chalkboards, flip charts, duplicated material, slides, transparencies, videotape, computer art, CDs, DVDs, and audio aids.

Visual aids should be easily and clearly seen by the audience, should be easy for the speaker to manipulate, should accurately represent the concept being discussed, and should be free of distracting elements. In short, a visual aid should aid, not detract. Practice using visual aids before making a speech. During the presentation, remember to look at the audience (not the visual aid), synchronize the visual aids with what is being said, do not block the audience's view of the aid, and display only one at a time.

Concepts and Questions

1. What are the major advantages of using visual aids when giving a speech?

2. What are some of the factors that should be considered when selecting a visual aid?

3. Name and describe five types of visual aids.

4. As it relates to this chapter, explain the statement "A picture is worth a thousand words."

Activities and Exercises

1. Bring four visual aids to class and explain each of them in light of the material discussed in this chapter.

2. Watch four television commercials. Make a list of the types of visual aids the makers of the commercial used to make their point.

3. Take a trip to the media center on campus and examine the catalogues that list various films, videos, CDs, DVDs, and so on. Determine the type of equipment available for student check out.

4. Give a humorous speech demonstrating some of the problems that might occur when using visual aids. ✦

Chapter 7

Presenting the Message

Managing Voice and Body

How you present your information is what first and foremost influences the audience. Regardless of how much research you have conducted or how honorable your objective, the *presentation*, or delivery, is what brings a speech to life. Unless the delivery is dynamic and skillful, it will detract from the overall message and negate the ultimate objective. A good presentation can enliven even the dullest topic. Conversely, even a dynamic topic becomes monotonous if the presentation is uninspired.

The Importance of Delivery

There are a number of reasons that make speech delivery so important. First, the speaker's voice and body movements send ideas to the audience. As noted in Chapter 1, a sender's voice and actions are the channels that convey thoughts to another human being.

Second, the way nonverbal elements of voice and body are used influences the audience's perception of the speaker's credibility and effectiveness. When audience's assess credibility, the speaker's personal image and delivery are intertwined. Nothing hurts a speaker's image more than a dull, monotonous voice and listless body activity. If the speaker fails to exhibit enthusiasm, the audience will lack interest in both the speaker and the topic.

Third, speaker appearance is important because of the power of first impressions. Remember, the audience makes judgments about the speaker even before they hear the first words of a speech. Part of their decision will be based on the speaker's dress, accessories, and posture. Justly or unjustly, if listeners form an unfavorable impression, they may ignore the actual speech.

Fourth, nonverbal behaviors convey a strong emotional message. The face and body provide greater insight to one's emotional state than do words. Even voice inflections carry important messages. Because nonverbal communication is more universal than verbal communication, cultural barriers can often be bridged with actions such as smiling, pointing, and gesturing.

Messages are expressed by all parts of the body at the same time. Tone of voice, volume, pitch, and speaking rate occur simultaneously with movement, gestures, eye contact, and other nonverbal elements. Therefore, it is important for the speaker to ensure that these elements blend harmoniously.

This chapter, which explores some cultural variations that apply to nonverbal communication, serves two purposes. First, the information can help you adapt your delivery to culturally diverse audiences. Second, an awareness of cultural differences in nonverbal communication will enable you to appreciate and perhaps interpret those differences. However, unless a cultural variation is specified, we will discuss nonverbal behaviors as they tend to be viewed from a Euro-American perspective.

Visual Perceptions of the Speaker

Even before a single word is said, the speaker produces a number of visual signals that can affect the way the audience perceives and reacts to the presentation. These include, (1) general appearance, (2) facial expression, (3) eye contact, (4) body movement, and (5) use of space. An awareness of each element's role in influencing listener reaction can help obviate barriers to effective communication.

General Appearance

When preparing for an interview, you pay particular attention to your appearance. Why? Because you know that what people think of you is frequently based on how you look and act. Posture, clothes, jewelry and accessories, and general grooming all contribute to that critical first impression. A convincing appearance increases your chance of success. For the same reasons, appearance is an important consideration when giving a speech. The audience will see you before they hear you.

Posture communicates a great deal about a speaker. A rigid, stiff posture conveys tension, anxiety, and nervousness, while slouching suggests resignation, lack of enthusiasm, or perhaps boredom. Euro-Americans react most favorably to a speaker who appears comfortable and alert. Although no single posture is always right for all speakers on all subjects on all occasions, as a general guideline you should try to avoid the extremes of being too rigid or too sloppy. Strive for an even distribution of body weight so as to appear both poised and relaxed, while not appearing nonchalant.

What you wear also influences the audience. In every culture, the way people dress plays a role in how others perceive them. Rightly or wrongly, we initially judge people by their appearance. While it is difficult to prescribe the appropriate *apparel* for every situation, the successful communicator is able to adapt to the audience, the setting, and the speaking event. Also, remember that audience standards and judgments are a function of their culture. A dark suit, white shirt, and conservative tie would be appropriate in England, but an open-necked *barong* would be more acceptable for the Philippines. Ultimately, it is the speaker's responsibility to be aware of the audience's expectations, which should be learned in the audience analysis.

Facial expressions send multiple signals and depict a wide range of emotions, from fear to confidence and from joy to sadness. Drawing on observations of the speaker's facial expressions, listeners form impressions and personal opinions of the speaker's attitude toward the audience and the topic.

Culture, however, can play a role in the appropriateness or inappropriateness of facial expressions. Some cultures, such as Western Europeans and Americans, expect the face to exhibit a range of emotion. If the setting of the speech and ideas warrant it, the speaker should use a variety of facial expressions during a presentation to a Euro-American audience. In contrast, many Asian cultures see the outward display of emotion as childlike or even offensive. As in every situation, it is incumbent on the speaker to gain an awareness of the audience's expectations.

Some communication scholars maintain that **eye contact** is the most important aspect of delivery. The rationale is simple: the eyes are capable of sending innumerable messages. The eyes reflect emotional state, be it elation or depression, interest or boredom, trust or suspicion, love or hatred. During a communication interaction, eye contact also reveals information concerning status, relationships, interest, motivation, anxiety, and many other personal factors.

Three general guidelines about eye contact should be remembered when addressing Euro-Americans. First, you should establish eye contact with the audience before beginning to talk. Second, look at everybody. Finally, sustain eye contact with one person for a few seconds before moving to another member of the audience. In some settings, you may want to focus on a single individual and only occasionally scan across the rest of the audience, such as when your objective is to persuade and the senior audience member will make the final decision. When addressing someone of high status—e.g., a high-level government official or corporate executive—the majority of eye contact should be directed toward him or her.

These recommendations are, of course, culture bound. Some cultures, such as the Japanese, find sustained eye contact disconcerting or even threatening. It is also common for some Japanese audience members to listen with their eyes closed. A culturally informed speaker will know that this technique is used to enhance listening ability and that the audience is not really falling asleep. Here again, it is important for the speaker to know the audience's cultural norms.

Body Movement

Body movements can be intentional and planned to achieve a specific purpose, or unintentional and spontaneous, beyond one's immediate control. Whether deliberate or unplanned, all body movements send a message. Movements during communicative acts are a natural response to our own words, the reactions of the listener, and the influence of the occasion. In most informal situations, people use movement naturally, freely, and often subconsciously. Public-speaking situations, on the other hand, frequently impose restraints that inhibit the natural impulse to move. We anchor ourselves in one spot (usually behind a lectern) for the duration of the speech. We grip the lectern or thrust our hands in our pockets or otherwise immobilize them so they cannot be used for meaningful, spontaneous gestures. Thus, we deprive ourselves of an important means of reinforcing the verbal message and of successfully competing with the other stimuli fighting to gain the listeners' attention.

When circumstances suggest that meaningful bodily action will add impact to the verbal message, adopt a bodily position that encourages (or at least does not inhibit) easy, spontaneous movement. If the occasion calls for a formal, stand-up speech, your movements are likely to be limited to gestures. When you are in close proximity to the audience, changes in facial expression may be the only movements needed.

Most of us experience a number of inhibitions when we have to appear before an audience. We become tense, and our hands suddenly seem bound by an invisible force. Our first impulse is to get them out of sight, so we thrust them into our pockets (where they will probably jingle coins or keys), lock them behind our backs, clasp them together in front of us in the so-called fig-leaf position, or grip the lectern until our knuckles turn white. This can be one reason why it does not feel natural to gesture during a speech: we have placed our hands and ourselves in a position that inhibits natural, spontaneous movement. Just as it is wise to adopt a posture, or stance, that will not restrain movement from one location to another, it is also wise to adopt a position that does not hinder hand and arm movement. The best thing to do is to keep hands and arms unencumbered. Then, when you feel a spontaneous urge to gesture, your hands and arms can move into motion in a natural manner.

Here are a few guidelines for using movement in public speaking:

- *Body movement should be naturally occurring.* Do not force your movements. The audience can easily discern the difference between natural and forced body movements.

- *Body movement should not be overused.* If body movement is overworked, listeners will begin to focus on the actions rather than the message.

- *Body movement should be appropriate for the occasion.* Tailor body movement to the circumstances. In a large room, where there is some distance between the speaker and the most remote section of the audience, your movements need to be pronounced so everyone can see them clearly. If speaking in a small, intimate room, your movements should be more restrained (and probably fewer).

- *Body action should be appropriate to the audience.* Not all cultures use and interpret nonverbal behavior in the same manner. Therefore, normative body movements should be reviewed from the cultural perspective of the expected audience.

- *Body movement should not be random.* Subconscious, unrelated movement can distract the audience from the message. Hands in pockets jiggling keys or constantly touching your hair will eventually become an irritant to the listeners.

- *Body movement should not be one-dimensional.* Strive for variety in body movement. Attempt to vary gestures and try to alternate between walking and standing still.

Culture's Influence on Visual Aspects

Culture is all pervasive. It influences our behavior in both obvious and subtle ways. The same is true of the nonverbal influences that are part of one's cultural heritage, and some of those influences can be reflected in the public-speaking arena. Nonverbal behaviors frequently carry different meanings for different cultures. This is especially true of learned behaviors such as posture, dress, facial expressions, eye gaze, body movement, use of space, and vocal variation. The rules of the dominant American culture dictate when, where, and to whom we can show certain emotions. We normally interpret and assign meanings to another person's nonverbal behaviors based on what those behaviors mean in our culture. It is easy to see that misunderstandings can arise when people from different cultures engage in communication. An effective speaker must be aware of how the nonverbal aspects of his or her speech delivery can be interpreted by a multicultural audience.

Posture

The effect of culture on posture during communication can be seen in a variety of ways. Among Euro-Americans, being spontaneous and casual is highly valued. It is not uncommon to see speakers reflecting these characteristics in the way they stand and sit. However, in cultures that are more formal (e.g., German, English, Swedish, Japanese), being too relaxed can be perceived as disrespectful and even lower one's credibility. In highly formal cultures, even the simple act of placing one's hand in a pocket can be interpreted as a sign of indifference.

Cultures also differ in the body orientations they display during communication activities. Anyone who has interacted with Arabs realizes that they use a very direct body orientation when communicating. The Chinese, on the other hand, tend to feel uncomfortable with this style and will usually communicate in a less direct stance, particularly with strangers.

Apparel

Clothing is also a reflection of both cultural values and a culture's approach to communication. In cultures where formality is valued, relaxed dress is seldom worn in professional settings. In the Arab, Mexican, English, and German cultures, formal attire is appropriate even in very warm weather. When addressing an audience composed of members from these cultures, it is best to dress in a formal, conservative manner.

Facial Expressions

How facial expressions are displayed is also subject to the dictates of culture. In public, for example, Koreans, Japanese, and Chinese do not normally exhibit facial expressions as outward signs of emotion. In fact, in these cultures people have learned to mask their emotions. Some Japanese will even go so far as to hide expressions of anger, sorrow, or disgust by laughing or smiling. Emotions are usually reserved for intimate friends and family members and are expressed in private.

In many Mediterranean cultures, however, people take a very different view of facial expressions. There, both men and women will be very animated when speaking, and they expect others to be equally emotive. In the United States, some groups use facial expressions in ways that differ from that of the majority of the population. Some American Indian groups, for example, use far less facial animation than other Americans do. Evidence also suggests that women use more facial expressions and smile more than men.

The smile is another nonverbal expression rooted in culture. Even though smiling is a universal facial expression, the amount of smiling, the stimulus that produces the smile, and even what the smile is communicating often vary from culture to culture. In the United States, a smile can be a sign of happiness or friendly affirmation when used with a greeting. But in Korean culture, too much smiling can be perceived as a sign of a shallow or insincere person. What is important about these examples is that they call attention to the idea that to adapt delivery to meet specific cultural characteristics a speaker needs to know something about the cultural background of the audience members.

Eye Contact

Although people everywhere use eye contact for similar reasons, cultural norms govern the amount of eye contact a person can engage in and with whom. In the United States, people expect direct, eye-to-eye contact with their communication partners and tend to be suspicious of anyone who does not look them in the eye. In certain other cultures, however, direct eye contact may be interpreted as a sign of disrespect or hostility. The Chinese, Koreans, and Japanese usually avoid sustained eye contact. Some Nigerians and Puerto Ricans have been raised to think that prolonged gazes are impertinent. The same sort of socialization process often has Latino children avoiding eye contact as a sign of respect. At the other end of the spectrum, Arab culture subscribes to direct and prolonged eye gaze as a sign of showing interest in the communication partner.

How men and women of a culture relate to one another also has implications for eye contact. In some Middle Eastern cultures, women are not expected to look directly into the eyes of men. Accordingly, the men of those cultures respectfully avert their eyes from the women, in contrast to the directness of their gaze at other men. French, Italian, and Argentine men, however, have no inhibitions about staring openly at women. Gender also plays a role in the use of eye contact, as some studies indicate that American women maintain more eye contact and hold eye contact longer with their communication partners than do American men.

So delicate is the use of eye contact that we seldom realize the modifications we make. For example, the next time you are talking to a physically challenged person, perhaps someone in a wheelchair, notice how little eye contact you make with him or her as compared with someone who is not physically challenged. An effective public speaker will be aware of these nuances in eye contact in order to include everyone in the audience in his or her gaze.

Movement

Our earlier discussion of movement focused on its application to the dominant U.S. culture. But what is normal for Euro-Americans may vary significantly in another culture. In some cultural groups (e.g., Arab, Israeli, Italian), the norm is a great deal of activity and animation. In many other cultures (e.g., Japanese, English, German), people are expected to be reserved in both manner and movement. There are even cultural differences in greeting behaviors. Someone from Japan might bow as a way of first addressing an audience, while a person from India would find it appropriate to perform the *namaste* by placing both hands together in front of his or her chest and inclining the head and shoulders slightly forward, while saying *namaste*. It is important to be aware of cultural variations as you move from audience to audience.

We can also observe significant differences in the use of gestures by looking at co-cultures in the United States. African Americans, because they value a lively and expressive communication style, display a much greater variety of movements when communicating than do whites. Also as compared to males, women tend to use fewer and smaller gestures.

Space

The way people use and respond to space is shaped by cultural orientation. People from individualistic cultures frequently demand more personal space than people from collectivist cultures. Thus, two friends conversing in the United States, Germany, Scotland, or Sweden might sit or stand farther apart than their counterparts in Israel, Greece, Mexico, Italy, or Brazil. It is common for students in Asian cultures to stand farther away from their teachers than U.S. students do. This added distance reflects respect for the teacher. The successful public speaker must be aware of these differences when moving toward members of the audience. Some people may welcome the closeness while others might feel uncomfortable or even threatened.

Aural Dimensions of Presentation

Your voice does a lot more than simply make words audible to the audience; it enables you to infuse those words with different shades of meaning. The voice, like posture, gestures, facial expressions, and body movements, tells things about the speaker quite apart from the verbal message. Thus, an effective speaker is mindful of the voice's potential to help or hinder communication.

Vocal Variation

Vocal variety can help sustain audience attention. A speaker who fails to vary voice pitch, loudness, or rate will have difficulty maintaining audience attention for any length of time. Vocal effectiveness depends, largely, on the way you control loudness (volume), pitch, quality, rate, distinctness (articulation), and correctness (pronunciation).

1. *Loudness* (volume). The first requisite of vocal sound is that it be loud enough for comfortable hearing. Although attaining a sufficient volume is the first concern, the need for changes in volume is also an important factor. By varying loudness and having a great deal of vocal variety, you can enhance word meaning, impart emphases to words or phrases, and sustain audience attention.

2. *Pitch.* Changes in pitch level (inflection in upward and downward movement) provide an effective means of imparting different shades of meaning to spoken words. Moreover, such changes tend to help sustain audience attention.

3. *Rate.* Comprehension, meaning, and attention are all affected by how fast a speaker talks. If the speaker talks too fast, the audience may have difficulty in understanding the message. If the rate is slow when it should be fast or fast when it should be slow, meaning may suffer. If the rate is not correctly varied, audience attention may wane. A *pause* can also be used to manage rate and, when used effectively, is an excellent vocal device. However, many inexperienced speakers often fill the pause with what are called vocal interferences, or disfluencies, such as "uh," "ah," "er," "um," "well," "OK," "like," and "you know." Such disfluences should always be avoided.

4. *Distinctness* (articulation). Success as a public speaker is directly linked to the clarity, or distinctness, of the sounds produced. The way words are articulated and enunciated influence the audience's perception of the speaker's credibility and the meaning of the speech.

5. *Pronunciation.* While enunciation concerns the distinctness of a spoken word, pronunciation has to do with correctness. Listeners are less likely to forgive faults of pronunciation than faults of enunciation, because faulty pronunciation is sometimes considered a reflection of the speaker's intelligence and educational level. If doubts arise regarding the correct pronunciation of any word, consult a dictionary that offers guidelines for pronunciation. Some online dictionaries, such as Merriam-Webster OnLine (<http://www.m-w.com/dictionary.htm>) offer audible pronunciation prompts.

In an era of increased intercultural interaction, accents are another important consideration in pronunciation. For many people,

English is a second language and levels of fluency vary widely. As listeners, we are obligated to manifest a high degree of intercultural awareness, sensitivity, tolerance, and patience when being addressed by a non-native English speaker.

Dialects

A dialect represents a language variant used by a collection of people from a similar geographic region or ethnic background. Dialects can be troublesome in public speaking because listeners may make a positive or negative judgment based on the speaker's dialect. Although such reactions are unavoidable, it is important to remember that there is no such thing as a correct or incorrect dialect, or accent. This is especially true in the United States, where so many dialects are spoken, some of which are peculiar to a specific geographic region. What is standard in New Orleans might not be understandable in Milwaukee or Seattle.

People who share a common cultural background often have a distinctive dialect. Not only is their pronunciation of some words different from that of the majority of the people in a geographic area, but their grammar and syntax may differ as well. The dialects of Hispanic Americans, African Americans, and Asian Americans are cases in point. Each group has its own standards of pronunciation, grammar, and syntax for communication within their respective groups. But when they interact with members of the larger community, or dominant culture, which has other communicative norms, they face the problem of deciding which set of standards to follow—the ethnic standard or the majority standard. In such communication encounters, someone adhering to the ethnic standard runs the risk of being perceived by some culturally uninformed members of the majority culture as inarticulate. However, if the norms set by the cultural majority are followed, someone from a minority group may be considered disloyal or arrogant by members their own culture.

As intercultural understanding increases, respect for the speech patterns of others also grows. Moreover, with increasing social mobility and the pervasiveness of mass communication, regional and cultural differences in pronunciation are becoming less evident, and most people no longer see dialects as indicators of social position or educational achievement.

Aural Dimensions and Culture

You should never be quick to equate someone's voice with his or her character or emotional state. You have to consider the possibility that the speaker may be observing cultural norms that differ from your own. For instance, the Japanese sometimes use laughter to mask disapproval, embarrassment, sadness, and even anger. Thus, we need to be wary of making snap judgments about others based on their vocal behavior.

Volume, either loud or soft, is a case in point. For example, Israelis, Italians, and Arabs tend to speak loudly and can even convey the impression, at least to those who do not understand these cultures, of shouting. This intensity of volume is in stark contrast to what is found among American Indians and East Asians, who generally speak in much softer tones. Imagine the potential for misunderstanding that can arise when people of diverse cultures attempt to interact. For example, in Thailand, where a soft-spoken voice is the norm, a loud-spoken Euro-American might be perceived as angry or disturbed about something. Discovering the audience's cultural composition will help you to adapt your vocal volume to the audiences' cultural expectations.

Pitch is another vocal characteristic influenced by culture. Arabic speakers, for example, are often perceived to speak in an unusually high pitch, which can be misinterpreted as a display of intense emotion. There are also cultural differences in the use and perception of long pauses. For many Euro-Americans, an extended pause can cause tension, anxious feelings, and discomfort, so drawn-out pauses are avoided. In India, Japan, and among the Navaho, there is less uneasiness with silence and long pauses. For members of those cultures, a prolonged pause is perceived as a time for reflection and the gathering of one's thoughts—it sends a positive message, not a negative one.

These examples point out the importance of becoming aware of cultural differences in how people use their voices. You must be careful not to apply the dominant Euro-American standards to other cultures, which can lead to misinterpretations and misunderstandings.

Improving Delivery

Drawing on our discussion of the various components of speech delivery and how they can be influenced by culture, we will now offer some suggestions on how to apply that information. The following recommendations offer a succinct guide to help you improve your delivery when addressing a predominantly Euro-American audience. Ideas applicable to a multicultural audience are offered in the section following this one.

Body Movement

- Practice good posture.
- Dress appropriate for the occasion and the audience.
- Be enthusiastic.
- Maintain a pleasant, positive facial expression.
- Establish and maintain good eye contact with the audience.
- Use meaningful gestures to reinforce points.
- Move about to emphasize a point or make a transition.
- Avoid standing too close to, or far away, from the audience.

Voice

- Cultivate vocal variety.
- Enunciate clearly.
- Pronounce words correctly.
- Analyze and evaluate delivery practices in various communication situations.

Self-confidence

The speaker's self-confidence levels can be greatly increased by:

- Knowing the subject and outline.
- Allowing sufficient time to practice.
- Developing a positive mental attitude toward the speaking occasion.
- Being enthusiastic about the topic.

Addressing the Multicultural Audience

We have provided many examples of how communicative behaviors and styles differ among cultures and how you, as a speaker, might adjust your presentation to fit those differences. However, our recommendations have tended to assume that most audience members were from the same or a similar culture. Of course, in the United States you will rarely have a culturally homogenous audience. The ethnically varied demographics almost guarantee that your audience will come from a variety of cultural backgrounds. Moreover, the individual members may be at different stages of adaptation to the dominant cultural norms. Some may be first- or second-generation Americans and still have strong ties to their culture of origin. Others, who can trace their American roots over several generations, may have become completely assimilated to the dominant culture and possess only a weak or topical association to their ethnic culture.

This situation raises the question, "How do I adapt my speech to a multicultural audience?" Unfortunately, there is no easy or simple answer to this question. On some occasions, adjusting your presentation to fit the cultural norms of one group may be counterproductive to members of another group. Thus, your audience analysis becomes increasingly important when scheduled to address multicultural listeners. To help you with the dilemma of talking to a group of listeners from diverse cultural backgrounds, we offer the following recommendations.

- Try to present a conservative appearance unless you know the occasion will be informal. It is always safer to overdress than to underdress.

- Until you can get a sense of expectation from the audience, adhere to a formal format. If, during the speech, you determine that the occasion and the audience are more relaxed, you can make the necessary adjustments.

- Continually self-monitor your nonverbal activity and try to avoid any exaggerated facial expressions or body movements. Maintain a pleasant expression and employ a constant eye scan of the audience, avoiding focusing too long on any single individual.

- Adjust your speaking rate to fit the audience's comprehension level. If English is the second language of most listeners, you should consider speaking more slowly, using short pauses, restating the most important points, and avoid overly complex terms, slang, and regional expressions. This approach will allow your audience time to think about what you have just said and reduce the chance of misunderstandings.

- Select your metaphors carefully. They may not translate across cultural borders.

- Be careful with humor. What is amusing in one culture can be offensive in another.

Above all else, be constantly mindful. Speaking to a multicultural audience can be particularly challenging. You will need to be extra sensitive in monitoring audience feedback during the actual presentation, and be prepared to make adjustments in response to the listeners' reactions throughout the speech.

Chapter Summary

For effective oral communication, it is essential that the verbal and nonverbal elements of the message work in harmony. The nonverbal elements of the message are visual and vocal. The visual components include the speaker's general appearance (posture and apparel), facial expressions, eye contact, movements, and spatial relationship to the audience. The speaker's appearance should provide nonverbal cues that are compatible with the spoken message. Movements help convey meaning and sustain audience attention. The speaker should adopt a body position that does not inhibit spontaneous movement. Movement on the platform is generally motivated by a desire to emphasize an idea or to suggest a transition from one idea to another. The amount of space between the speaker and listener can affect the quality of the communication encounter. A speaker should use spatial cues in a manner consistent with the speech purpose.

The voice enables a speaker to impart various shades of meaning to the spoken word; it transmits an impression of the speaker as a person and acts as a factor of attention. The controllable elements of voice are loudness, pitch, and rate. These components should be varied in a manner consistent with the desired importance of the verbal message. Faults in distinctness of vocal sounds (enunciation) are more readily forgiven than are faults in the correctness of the sounds (pronunciation). Acceptability of pronunciation varies from region to region. A successful speaker needs to be aware of the influence of culture on all aspects of nonverbal communication. When addressing a multicultural audience, be more self-aware of your personal appearance, your nonverbal actions, and conscious of your language usage.

Concepts and Questions

1. How can body movements help or hinder a presentation?

2. What elements of the voice are controllable?

3. What methods could you use to remain calm and relaxed while delivering a speech?

4. Why is eye contact such an important aspect of successful delivery?

5. What are some of the cultural factors to consider when analyzing nonverbal behaviors?

Activities and Exercises

1. Attend a public event where a speaker is addressing an audience. Write a short report analyzing the speaker's delivery style.

2. Make a video recording of your next speech. Review the video and write an essay discussing the manner in which you delivered the talk. In your analysis, include some of the elements discussed in this chapter.

3. Use a video recording (e.g., from C-SPAN) of a speaker who you believe possesses good delivery skills. Make a list of specific techniques the speaker used that you might be able to incorporate into your own presentations. For each technique, explain why you think speaker effectiveness was enhanced.

4. Prepare a 3–4 minute speech that discusses cultural differences in nonverbal communication. ✦

Chapter 8

Connecting Ideas in the Message

Introductions and Conclusions

In previous chapters, we focused on the most effective ways of arranging materials in order to clearly and directly support a presentation's main ideas as they are contained in the body of a speech. But what about the other two major parts of a presentation—the introduction and the conclusion? How do you introduce the body, the substance of the presentation, and how do you bring the speech to an effective conclusion? This chapter will help answer both of those questions as we now turn our attention to *introductions* and *conclusions*.

Preparing the Introduction

We have already mentioned in several previous chapters the important role of first impressions. This significance cannot be overstated. When you are first introduced to someone, you quickly form an opinion of the person based on your initial impression. The same thought process occurs in the public speaking setting. The **introduction**, or beginning, helps the speaker establish a positive image and capture the audience's attention. More specifically, a good introduction should (1) gain the listeners' attention, (2) motivate them to want to listen to the entire speech, (3) establish your goodwill and credibility, and (4) prepare the listeners for what is to follow. Although these four purposes are often combined, each helps to set the tone for the rest of the talk. The first part of this chapter explains how you can achieve these objectives at the beginning of a speech, while the last part discusses the functions of an effective conclusion.

Gaining Attention

In any communication situation, the speaker is confronted with countless distractions that compete for the audience's attention. The room can be too hot, outside noises can be disruptive, some audience members may be talking among themselves, and others may be enjoying a private daydream. It is easy enough to gain the audience's momentary attention by simply walking to the front of the room. The real task, however, is to capture the kind of favorable attention that attracts and holds the audience's interest throughout the presentation. The following are some proven methods to gain and maintain attention at the beginning of a talk.

Quotations. A favorite device for opening many speeches is a thought-provoking or curiosity-arousing quotation. The interest value of this technique is that someone else has previously made a striking observation about the issue to be discussed. For example, a speaker used the following to introduce a speech on the topic of cultural differences in doing business:

> There is an Arab proverb that states, "Live together like brothers, and do business like strangers."

This seemingly simple proverb offers great insight into how the Arab culture perceives the business arena.

Another speaker, whose topic centered on the contributions of Martin Luther King, Jr. to American culture and the history of racial equality, started with the following famous quotation:

> How many of you have heard these famous lines before? "I have a dream that one day this nation will rise up and live out the true meaning of its creed: 'We hold these truths to be self-evident: that all men are created equal.'. . . I have a dream that my four children will one day live in a nation where they will be judged not by the color of their skin but the content of their character: I have a dream today."

The reference section of any library carries books of sayings and quotations that can be used to support a speech on almost any topic. Collections of quotations on nearly every subject can also be found on the Internet using any major search engine.

Illustrations and Anecdotes. If properly handled, stories, anecdotes, and illustrations can be effective openings. Illustrations can
be factual or hypothetical. In a speech focusing on the dangers of
some commonly prescribed drugs, the speaker used the following
factual illustration to arouse interest and direct the talk to the central
point of the speech:

> It was to have been a very happy occasion for this young,
> newly married couple—their first New Year's Eve together.
> But on New Year's Eve morning last year, says Jerry Thomas,
> "I awoke to hear my wife Mary gasping for air. As Mary's
> entire body throbbed out of control, I dialed 911 and then
> began frantically blowing air into her lungs, but it was too
> late." At first the death of the healthy 22-year-old woman was
> a mystery. But just last month the mystery was solved. Mary's
> death certificate was stamped with the following words:
> "Death due to a toxic level of the antihistamine hismanal."

In a speech about preparing for earthquakes, a speaker stimulated interest by using a hypothetical illustration that made the
members of the audience the central characters of the story:

> Imagine you were sitting at home one night and suddenly
> felt a strange rocking sensation coming from your chair—a
> sensation strong enough that it forced to you to stop what
> you were doing. As you began to concentrate on what was
> happening you noticed two extraordinary occurrences—the
> pictures on the wall were moving, and your dog was howling
> in a manner you had never heard before. All at once it hit
> you—the movement and the howling were related. You were
> experiencing an earthquake. As you looked around the home
> and started to see objects flying in many directions, it quickly
> became clear that this was a very serious earthquake. One
> question seemed to be repeating itself in your head: "What
> should I do?" And now I ask you that question: "Would you
> know what to do if you were caught in a major earthquake?"

Before deciding to open a speech with a story or an illustration,
it is necessary to ensure that (1) it is fresh (old stories told from a
new slant can be as fresh as brand-new stories), (2) it is pertinent to
the main theme of the speech, (3) it can be effectively related (personal limitations as a storyteller should be considered), and (4) it is

not offensive. The importance of this last quality cannot be overemphasized and extends across issues of culture and gender.

Reference to Recent Event or Occasion. Associating the theme of a speech with something currently in the news is another good way to gain the audience's attention. For instance, a talk on the rising costs of prescription drugs could begin with a reference to a recent news event:

> Yesterday, the National Public Radio aired a program about U.S. citizens purchasing prescription drugs from Canada. Did you know that the city of San Francisco's official web site now has links to reputable Canadian drugstores?

Connecting your presentation with some current event or activity imparts an air of freshness and immediacy that is likely to make the audience want to hear more. Referring to a contemporary event or occasion is an excellent technique for formal presentations, such as a banquet, a graduation ceremony, a dedication, or any situation where the occasion is the primary reason people have gathered. For example, "We are all here tonight to pay tribute to a woman who has made a difference in our community" would be an appropriate way to begin a speech at an appreciation banquet.

Rhetorical Question. When a speaker poses a rhetorical question, it "forces" the listener to want the answer. A skillfully phrased question creates a feeling of suspense that makes the audience want to "stay tuned." However, not just any question will do; it must make the audience eager for an answer. Lacking that element, a rhetorical question will be ineffectual as an attention device. Naturally, what makes an audience curious for an answer depends on the nature of that particular group of listeners. A group of entering freshmen at an orientation meeting would probably be attentive if the dean of admissions asked: "How many of you will still be in college next year to start your sophomore year?" A question of this nature would command far less attention from a group of university seniors.

Startling Statement or Fact. A startling statement can be useful when introducing a speech on a familiar theme, such as urging people to wear seat belts. In such cases, the speaker can incorporate listeners into a startling statement. For instance a speech on long-term healthcare could begin by using a statement that personalizes the information for the audience members.

Isn't it too bad about these three people sitting in the front row? They are going to be hospitalized for quite a while—probably long enough to exhaust all their savings. They may have to sell everything they own—car, furniture, even their homes.

Because many introductions work in combination, on some occasions a startling statement takes the form of a rhetorical question: "How many of you realize that the United States, with only 5 percent of the world's population, generates more greenhouse emissions than any other country on earth?" To be effective, the startling statement or fact must be relevant to the topic and should be based on an understanding of the audience. Here again we see the importance of the audience analysis.

Humor. If relevant to the topic and done in good taste, humor can get a speech off to an excellent start, but the humor must point the audience in the direction of the topic. In the following illustration, the speaker planned to talk about cultural differences in the use of language. To arouse attention while introducing the topic, she used the following opening:

A Frenchman studying English indicated he found English to be a strange language. He had to ask his teacher, "What does this mean—'Should Congresswoman Noble, who sits for this constituency, consent to stand again, she will in all probability have a walkover?' "

Visual and Audio Aids. Visual aids, as previously discussed, can both clarify an idea and stimulate interest, a twofold advantage that makes them excellent devices for beginning a speech. A few examples from student speeches using visual aids will demonstrate the utility of these tools.

For a speech dealing with the earliest stages of organized culture, a student projected a transparency of a 40,000-year-old mural from a subterranean cave in France. In an effort to persuade an audience that schools need to teach more geography, a student placed a map on the board and asked the audience whether they could identify the 10 major countries outlined on the map. Finally, in a speech dealing with how women are portrayed in rap music, a student began by playing several rap videos. As you might suspect, these approaches captured everyone's attention.

Guidelines in Using Introductions

The following are several ideas that should help you in the preparation and delivery of the introduction to your presentation.

1. *Be creative.* Do not leap to the first introduction that comes to mind. Ask whether the introduction will make the audience stop what they are doing and focus on the speech.

2. *Prepare the introduction only after working on the body of the talk.* An idea for a compelling, interesting introduction will often emerge from the body of the speech.

3. *Avoid beginning with an apology.* An apology is appropriate in cultures such as the Japanese, but it is not a useful device in the United States, where opening with an apology can lower speaker credibility. Little sympathy will be elicited by telling the audience you did not have much time to prepare or that you do not know much about the subject. Humility is not a salient characteristic of the Euro-American culture.

4. *Do not make the introduction too brief.* A good introduction is intended to arouse attention and concurrently provide a moment that allows the audience to cease what they were doing and begin to focus on the speaker. This redirection of attention may take a few moments, and the introduction furnishes that time.

Preparing the Audience for the Speech

After gaining the audience's attention, the speaker must prepare them for what is to come. On many occasions they will have an idea of the topic based on the material included in the introduction. However, under normal circumstances, the introduction should accomplish one or more of the following tasks in order to adequately prepare the audience: (1) justify the topic, (2) focus the topic, (3) establish speaker credibility, (4) define terms, and (5) create a common ground with the audience. Depending on the time allotted, the type of speech being presented, the audience composition, and the topic, some of these tasks can be combined.

Justifying the Topic

When an audience has not gathered for the specific purpose of hearing a talk about a given topic, the speaker needs to offer them a reason for listening:

> Having listened to me for the last few minutes, you are aware that I am going to talk about how large agribusiness corporations brought about the demise of many family farms in the United States. Perhaps you are now saying, "Why should I listen?" Well, let me tell you why this topic concerns you.

The speaker then demonstrates why the topic is relevant to this particular audience.

In speeches to inform, the justification of the topic usually deals with the question, "Why do you need this information?" In a speech to persuade, it answers questions such as "How does this issue affect you?" and "Why should you be concerned about this problem and its solution?"

Focusing the Topic

It is often necessary to draw boundaries when discussing certain topics. For example, telling an audience, "Today I'm going to talk about AIDS," may well create more confusion than clarification. Will the talk discuss treatment methods? Future research directions? Legislative efforts to require universal testing for AIDS? Where AIDS is most frequently encountered? The availability of AIDS medication in underdeveloped nations? In such cases, it is important to point out what will be excluded as well as what is to be included in the speech. Doing so enables listeners to adjust their expectations accordingly. An audience that knows the topic's boundaries can listen more efficiently.

Establishing Credibility

If the audience is unaware of the speaker's authority (credibility) on a subject, it must be established during the early part of the speech. On some occasions the person introducing the speaker will outline the speaker's credentials. However, if the introducer fails to do so (or if there is no speaker introduction), the task falls on the speaker to make his or her credentials known. This task can usually be accomplished without creating an impression of immodesty. Following are a few examples:

> I want to share with you some information about Chinese immigration to the United States in the 1800s that I learned in my American history class last semester.

> You have read and heard about the dangerous aspects of street gangs. From second- and third-hand sources, you have been exposed to the violence associated with gangs. Well, I was a gang member in junior and senior high school, so I can tell you first-hand about this lifestyle. I know from my own experiences why people join gangs and how they can get out of them. Let me share some of these observations with you during the next 10 minutes.

> Last semester, I attended classes at a university in Madrid, Spain. I was one of only five American students in the entire school of 11,000 students. During that period, I lived with a Spanish family and had to speak Spanish every day. It was a demanding but rewarding experience. Today, I would like to share some of my insights about the best ways of adjusting to another culture.

Defining Terms

Some topics involve special terminology, jargon, or technical vocabulary that needs to be defined early in the speech. One student, speaking on the importance of proper eye care, defined *myopia*, *hyperopic*, *astigmatism*, *cataracts*, and *glaucoma* during the introductory portion of the talk. Terms can be defined in the introduction or when they are first used in the speech. When you are talking to a culturally diverse audience, defining terms and concepts takes on added significance.

Establishing Common Ground

Sometimes a speaker is forced to take an unpopular stand on a controversial issue. On these occasions, a special effort must be made to gain audience support. One method is for the speaker to establish a common ground of belief with the listeners. Essentially, it means taking steps to stress the areas of speaker-audience agreement before turning to the issues of speaker-audience disagreement. For instance, if you were eventually going to advocate that people on snowmobiles should no longer use certain areas of Yellowstone National Park, you might want to begin by talking about what is happening to the plants, animals, and air quality in the park. By establishing a common interest in the environment, you might be building common ground.

Introductions and Culture

By now it should be clear that that not every culture approaches communication in the same manner, nor do they necessarily have the same communication patterns. The topic of introductions is a clear example of how culture and communication are interrelated. As noted earlier, the whole idea of a speech having an introduction, a body, and a conclusion is a Western concept. In many cultures, people simply start talking without any concern for having to gain attention and interest. The following three cultural variations in starting a speech illustrate the role of culture in forming introductions.

First, in Japan, where modesty and humbleness is highly valued, it is not uncommon for a talk to begin with an apology. To reflect a deferential attitude, a speaker may start by implying that she wishes she could have had more time to prepare or that she hopes the speech will benefit the listeners. If your audience is composed of many people from Japan, you might attempt to offer this mild apology as part of the introduction:

> Thank all of you for taking time from your busy schedule to attend today's presentation. Unfortunately, since I do not speak Japanese, I must rely on English. My apologies.

In Latin American cultures, establishing rapport and feeling comfortable with the people you are around is very important. Hence, when talking to people from Mexico or any other Latin culture, it would be wise to spend some time putting everyone in a relaxed and amiable mood before beginning the body of the talk.

Third, in Western cultures, people often admire the speaker who is witty and clever, has a keen sense of humor, and can begin a speech with a joke. However, while laughter is universal, many cultures believe that the telling of jokes is the domain of the professional comedian, not the public speaker. They believe that people get paid for telling jokes and that the occasion of speechmaking is a more serious matter. Additionally, as we have preciously disclosed, humor often fails to travel across cultural borders.

Preparing the Conclusion

Unfortunately, speeches often end with these or similar words: "Well, I guess that's about all." Judge for yourself whether this ending accomplishes the desired functions of a speech **conclusion**: (1) Does it redirect the audience's attention to the central point of the speech and tie together the main content of the speech? (2) Does it move the listener into the frame of mind that should be dominant at the end? (3) Does it leave the listener with a sense of completeness?

There is a tendency for beginning speakers to give less thought to the preparation of the conclusion than to any other portion of the speech, yet the ending can be a critical part of the presentation. A poor conclusion can undermine everything the speaker has accomplished up to that point. Therefore, it is important to explore some of the ways to effectively close a speech.

Summarizing

A brief recapitulation, or **summary**, of the main points of the speech is a common concluding device. It is particularly valuable in instructional speeches because it reinforces the directions that the speaker wants the audience to recall. For example, in concluding a speech on the fundamentals of tennis, a speaker could use a summary in the following manner: "Today you learned some of the elementary techniques of tennis; when you're on the court, try to remember that (1) you should always keep your eye on the ball, (2) you should keep your arm firm, and (3) your swing should follow through." One speaker, informing the audience about the dangers and treatment of prostate cancer ended with this summary:

> Today, we learned that after skin cancer, prostate cancer is the number one cancer among men in the United States. The American Cancer Institute estimates that over 234,000 men will be diagnosed with prostate cancer in 2006, and more than 27,000 will die from the disease. But as we discussed, there are a variety of proven treatments, which include aggressive watchfulness, surgery, radiation therapy, and hormone therapy.

In persuasive speeches, a summary can remind listeners that sound reasons have been given to support the rationale the speaker has advanced or for the action that has been advocated.

Using Quotations

We have already seen that a quotation can serve as an effective opening of a speech; it can, with equal effectiveness, be part of the conclusion. One speaker, talking about the difficulties in understanding other cultures, ended with the following famous quotation by the English author Rudyard Kipling:

> Oh East is East, and West is West, and never the twain shall meet, Till Earth and Sky stand presently at God's great Judgment Seat.

Using an Illustration or Story

Like a quotation, an illustration can be used as effectively in the conclusion as in the introduction. Illustrations distill the essence of the message and present it in a form that makes it memorable to listeners. If the prevailing mood of the speech has been serious, the speaker might use an illustration or a story in a light vein to provide the touch needed to leave the audience in the right frame of mind. A student concluded a speech dealing with cultural differences in the perception of death with the following humorous anecdote:

> One of the main points of my speech is that cultures do not agree on what happens at the end of life. Well, cultures are not alone; most individuals don't know for sure about an afterlife. Comedian George Burns worked for over 30 years with his wife, Gracie Allen. After her death, he visited her grave regularly. Someone once asked him if he told Gracie what was going on in his life? "Sure, why not?" was his reply. "I don't know whether she hears me, I have never been dead, but I've nothing to lose, and it gives me a chance to break in new material."

Making a Challenge

Speeches designed to stimulate the audience to greater efforts or stronger devotion to a cause or an ideal often conclude with a challenge: "If we all work together, we can stop urban sprawl and keep the land developers from making our city one large parking lot and shopping mall. I implore you to help me preserve the little bit of open space we have left in our town." The challenge should be worded so as to encourage a spirit of confidence in the audience's capacity to meet the challenge. One of the most famous uses of the challenge was that issued by John F. Kennedy in his 1960 inaugural address, the much quoted "Ask not what your country can do for you—ask what you can do for your country."

Declaring Intent

Speeches intended to promote action can be ended effectively when the speaker sets an example for the audience by declaring what she or he personally plans to do.

> I will be the first one. I have now fastened a donor symbol to my driver's license. In the event of an emergency, this lets medical workers know my organs are available for donation. Please join me in this action so that other people can enjoy life after you are gone.

Referring to the Introduction

Returning to the introduction of the speech is often an effective method of concluding a talk. The introduction can be reestablished in a variety of ways. For example, if you started with a rhetorical question, you might end by restating the same question, but now offering the answer:

> Ten minutes ago, I asked if you knew what to do if an earthquake were to take place at this instant. Now, when I ask that question, the answer should be "yes."

Guidelines in Using Conclusions

When planning the conclusion, keep some of the following ideas in mind.

1. *Practice the conclusion so that it does not wander aimlessly.* Too many speakers fail to develop a concise conclusion and thus end up dragging it out for a long period as they drone on about insignificant issues.

2. *Avoid ending too abruptly.* Some speakers fail to prepare an effective conclusion and end without giving the audience any warning.

3. *Try not to add any new points.* If something is simply tossed in at the end, it will only confuse the audience and detract from the specific purpose.

4. *Stress the strongest ideas.* Remember that your conclusion will be the last thing the audience hears before you sit down.

5. *Avoid ending with an apology.* As already stated, in the dominant culture of the United States apologies can reduce your credibility. An apology should be considered only if your audience analysis suggests it would be appropriate.

Chapter Summary

After designing the body of the speech, the speaker must give considerable thought to the introduction and conclusion. An introduction gains attention and prepares the audience for the remainder of the speech. Among the methods of gaining attention are quotations, illustrations or stories, references to recent events or occasions, rhetorical questions, startling statements, humor, and visual aids. An introduction also justifies and delimits the topic, offers an opportunity to present the speaker's credentials, defines key terms, and establishes common ground.

The conclusion redirects the audience's attention to the core statement and tries to give the listeners a sense of completeness. Some methods of concluding are summary, quotation, illustration or story, challenge, declaration of intent, and reference to the introduction.

Concepts and Questions

1. What should the introduction accomplish?

2. Why is it important to have a good introduction?

3. Why is it important to have a good conclusion?

4. What is the rationale behind using rhetorical questions as a device for beginning a speech?

5. Why is it beneficial to restate your main points in the summary?

Activities and Exercises

1. Locate three quotations for a speech dealing with "cultural diversity."

2. Write three rhetorical questions for any of the following topics:

    a. Study habits.

    b. Adaptation to another culture.

    c. Study abroad programs.

3. Listen to a political speaker. Write a short essay discussing the speaker's introduction and conclusion.

4. Give a two-minute speech that begins with some form of humor. ✦

Chapter 9

Sharing the Message

The Informative Speech

The ability to render an idea clear and comprehensible is one of the most highly prized skills a person can possess in our complex, dynamic, information-oriented society. Being able to tell others, in a clear and interesting manner, how something functions or operates is considered the mark of an educated person. Regardless of the culture, individuals who possess knowledge, and an ability to share it, are perceived as being productive and credible. Having the ability to effectively inform others will give you a considerable advantage in any chosen endeavor.

Situations calling for the use of informative discourse are numerous and varied. Virtually all teaching can be labeled informative speaking. Instructing and training workforce, office, and sales staffs also involves informative speaking. A doctor outlining procedures to a surgical team preparing for a heart transplant must use informative communication. People engage in informative speaking at all levels of communication, both formal and informal. The "Information Age" has accelerated an unprecedented explosion of ideas and information; new concepts are emerging from every direction and from every discipline. Knowing how to organize, clarify, and transmit those concepts, particularly across cultural boundaries, has dramatically increased the role of informative speaking.

We have established that informative speaking is important, but what exactly does it do? The objective of an informative speech is to convey information that will increase audiences' knowledge about a particular subject. The primary goal is to present the information in a manner that makes it easily understood, remembered, and perhaps even applied by the listeners.

In this chapter, we will discuss the various types of informative speeches, outline the steps involved in preparing a talk to inform, and provide an example outline. You may find some of the information repetitive from previous chapters. However, earlier discussions focused on various parts of a presentation without providing a complete context. In examining the informative speech, we will bring all of the parts of a speech together, enabling you to see how everything is combined into a complete, coherent presentation.

Types of Informative Speeches

While all informative speeches have a common goal—to increase the audience's level of knowledge—they can take one of several different forms. Although in some instances the categories may overlap, it is useful for speakers to be aware of the distinguishing characteristics of the four basic types—instructive, descriptive, explanatory, and report.

Instructive

The most commonly used informative talk is the **instructive speech**, one that provides instructions or directions, often called the "how to" or "demonstration" speech. In an informative presentation, the speaker tells the audience the method for performing a particular task, such as how to install a new computer software program. During training classes, employers use instructional speeches to show new employees how to perform their job assignments. Some other "how to" subjects include:

- How to prepare for an emergency evacuation of your home in the event of a natural disaster.

- How to prepare for a job interview.

- How to apply for permanent alien residency (i.e., a green card).

- How to prepare *carne asada.*

Descriptive

The **descriptive speech** is used to describe something. Engineers, teachers, doctors, sales managers, and supervisors are often called on to describe a new model, a layout, a display, a location, an event, or even an attitude. To have the audience gain greater insight into the Prophet Mohammed, you might describe his family, his education, and his conversion to religion. Sample topics that would use description include:

- The Mexican "Day of the Dead" celebration.

- A mule ride to the bottom of the Grand Canyon.

- Food markets in rural India.

- Construction secrets of China's Great Wall.

Explanatory

The third general type of informative speech is **explanatory**— sometimes called *exposition*. Such speeches attempt to explain how and why an object, a process, or a procedure operates as it does. A speech discussing the principles of Darwin's theory of evolution would be an explanatory talk. Other examples of explanatory speeches are:

- To explain how the Internet works.

- To explain the effects of overdevelopment on the environment.

- To explain how the federal deficit is calculated.

- To explain the impact of greenhouse gasses.

Report

Almost everyone has been asked to present a **report** of some type. Perhaps it was a high school book report, a budget report, or a status report on a project. This speech involved transmitting to others the substance of what you had read, prepared, or accomplished. Here are some sample report speech topics:

- To report on plans for your city's participation in a Sister Cities cultural exchange program with an Italian city.

- To report on former President Bill Clinton's autobiography.

- To report on the security measures planned for the 2008 Olympic Games in Beijing, China.

- To report on legislation dealing with immigrants.

Despite their disparate objectives, each of the types of informative speeches shares a similar preparation process and organizational structure. The remainder of this chapter will concentrate on how to prepare an effective informative presentation.

Preparing a Speech to Inform

While being prepared is a useful trait for any effective form of communication, it is an extremely important aspect of public speaking. Good preparation involves research, analysis, and practice. Several general principles for preparing an informative speech warrant closer examination.

Identifying a Purpose

If the goal is to make ideas clear to others, you must first determine what the audience should know at the conclusion of the presentation. This is called the *specific purpose* and should be contained in a concise statement of exactly what you want the audience to understand. In the following examples of specific purpose statements, notice how each one states precisely what the speaker wants the listeners to comprehend:

- To have the audience understand the importance of recycling.

- To have the audience understand the importance of the extended family in Hispanic cultures.

- To have the audience understand how to request documents under the Freedom of Information Act.

Selecting and Focusing the Topic

Earlier in the book we talked about choosing and narrowing a topic for a speech. Let us briefly review some of these criteria:

- In most instances, *the speaker should know more about the topic than the audience members.* During the speech, modestly let the listeners know how you came to be knowledgeable about the subject being discussed.

- *The topic should be relevant.* Intelligent people do not like to hear about mundane subjects (e.g., how to frost a cake). A comprehensive audience analysis (coupled with common sense) will help avoid trite and uninteresting subjects.

- *The topic should be stimulating as well as timely.* The subject needs to arouse audience curiosity and then hold their attention.

- *Sufficient background material must be available.* Think how frustrating it would be if you decided to discuss effective multicultural educational practices in Afghanistan, only to discover that little or no information is available on this topic.

Selecting Supporting Material

An informative speech, like any presentation, requires reputable supporting material. The following five points should be used to guide your selection of credible reference materials:

- *Interest and clarity.* The speech should contain materials that are interesting, clear, and easily understood.

- *Audience involvement.* Select material that will mentally engage the audience and encourage them to take part in the communication process.

- *Audience analysis.* Be sure to keep the knowledge level and cultural backgrounds of the audience in mind when selecting material.

- *Visual aids.* Use graphics that allow the audience to see as well as hear the main points.

- *Variety in support materials.* Using varied support material (e.g., statistics, quotes, etc.) enhances audience understanding and helps maintain listener attention.

Organizing an Informative Speech

To be effective, a public speaker must have a plan. The systematic arrangement of material is crucial in informative speaking if the audience is to retain the data presented. Speeches that seem to jump from point to point seldom leave listeners with anything meaningful. Therefore, in this section, we examine the basic steps of organizing a speech to inform.

Introduction

The introduction to an informative speech has four interrelated purposes: (1) to arouse audience attention, (2) to create a desire for the more detailed information contained in the body of the speech, (3) to establish the speaker's credentials, and (4) to preview the main points of the speech.

Arouse Audience Attention. The various methods for starting a speech were discussed in Chapter 8, which highlighted the advantages of beginning a speech with a quotation, illustration, reference to a recent event, rhetorical question, startling statement, humor, or visual aids. You should review these techniques when preparing for an informative speech. Before deciding on a specific method for starting the talk, keep in mind the need to consider the topic, the audience's interest and knowledge level, the speaking time available, and the type of occasion.

Create a Desire to Listen. In all communication situations, it is advantageous to instill the audience with a desire to listen to the presentation. Therefore, it is important that the informative speech introduction clearly specify the topic as both significant and beneficial to the audience. For instance, a speaker could use the introduction to demonstrate that paying attention to the presentation could save listeners a great deal of money.

There are also occasions when interest can be aroused by appealing to the audience's curiosity. Think how intrigued you might be if a speaker began by telling a story of how the Tibetans dispose of their dead in ways very different from Western methods. A speaker who asked the audience if they knew where and how the AIDS epidemic began would also stimulate interest.

Establish the Speaker's Credentials. An informative speech is designed to increase the listeners' knowledge of a particular topic. The assumption is that the speaker knows something the audience does not and that, by listening, they will learn more about the subject. Thus, the third task of the informative introduction is to establish the speaker's personal credibility on the subject.

Preview Main Points. The final part of an introduction should provide a brief overview of the main points to be discussed in the body of the speech. The speaker addressing the origins of AIDS used the following preview to tell the audience what the speech would focus on:

In an effort to better understand the issue of AIDS, today I would like to begin by talking about the early cases of AIDS, then discuss the location of these early instances, and finally mention how AIDS has traveled throughout the world.

By providing a glimpse of the speech's organizational pattern, the speaker lets listeners know what to look for as the presentation progresses. If listeners are prepared for what is coming, they will find it much simpler to locate the main ideas.

On some occasions, it might even be useful to enumerate the organization by saying "first," "second," and "third" when summarizing the different sections. For example, a speaker talking about the history of AIDS could say, "I will talk first about where AIDS began, second about early AIDS cases, and third about the global spread of the disease."

Previews are also useful in laying a foundation for reinforcement and repetition—two processes important to learning. The preview is the first time the audience is introduced to the main points. As the speaker moves through the body of the speech and signposts each main idea, the audience hears the key points for a second time. Finally, in the summary at the conclusion, listeners are once again reminded of the main points. Hence, on three occasions, the main points are highlighted.

The same order should be followed in presenting information in the introduction, body, and conclusion of the speech. If the audience is told in the preview that the presentation will look at the advantages and then the disadvantages of the school voucher program, that order must not be reversed in either the body or the conclusion. While seemingly insignificant, such a change can confuse listeners.

Body

After completing the introduction, the speaker is ready to present the main body of information. Just as the introduction is organized into sections, the body of the speech must also be arranged into meaningful groupings. The division of the whole into its parts is an essential step in explaining any complex concept. The various elements are more easily remembered if they can be worded in a logical pattern or sequence. Let's reexamine some of the patterns of arrangement discussed in Chapter 5 to see how they can be applied to informative speaking.

Chronological Pattern. The chronological pattern has its greatest utility in presenting historical events, explaining processes, and relating personal experiences. A discussion of the history of voice recordings might develop material under these headings:

I. Cylinder recordings of the late 19th century.

II. Disk recordings of the early 20th century.

III. Long-play recordings of the mid-20th century.

IV. Compact disc recordings of the late 20th century.

V. Digital recordings of today.

Spatial Pattern. Spatial order is especially effective for speeches describing a scene, location, or geographical distribution. For instance, material can be arranged directionally from north to south, top to bottom, or center to outside. Weather patterns could be described according to those affecting the East Coast, Midwest, and West Coast. For a speech on how the Japan Current influences weather, the following order could be used:

I. Weather influences along the Japanese coast.

II. Weather influences along the Aleutian Islands.

III. Weather influences along the Alaskan Coast.

IV. Weather influences along the Pacific Coast.

Problem-Solution Pattern. The problem-solution sequence, a common organizational pattern for speeches to inform, moves the listeners from an obstacle (problem) to a remedy (solution). This sequence could be used to inform an audience about identity theft in the United States.

I. Identity theft is one of the fastest growing crimes in the United States.

II. All of us are vulnerable to identity theft.

III. There are several measures that will reduce your vulnerability to identity theft.

Ascending-Descending Pattern. The ascending-descending sequence takes listeners from the simple to the complex or from the less important to the more important. A speaker trying to explain the importance of various U.S. international trading partners could use the following ascending-descending (less important to more important) order:

I.   Tajikistan.

II. Honduras.

III. China.

IV. European Union.

V.   NAFTA

Causal Pattern. Causal order details causes of certain effects or explains the effects resulting from various causes. The following order could be used in a talk titled "What Are the Motivations for Illegal Immigration?"

I.   Political repression and illegal immigration.

II. Economic motivations behind illegal immigration.

III. Social marginalization and illegal immigration.

Using an examination of the relationship of illegal immigration with each of these conditions, a speaker could explain some of the causes that each year compels thousands of people to risk a perilous journey to illegally enter the United States.

Topical Pattern. The topical pattern is probably the most frequently used of all patterns for informational presentations. This arrangement sets out several facets of a topic that are obviously related and consistent. A talk about the financial structure of the Social Security system might include this pattern:

I.   Current assets of the Social Security system.

II. Current liabilities of the Social Security system.

III. Projected revenues of the Social Security system.

IV. Future liabilities of the Social Security system.

If speaking on the subject of the Islamic religion, the following topical pattern could be used:

I.   The history of Islam.

II. The role of the prophet Muhammad in Islam.

III. The Five Pillars of Islam.

IV. Islam in the modern world.

In the topical pattern, the structure should be rather apparent and one the audience most likely expects. The speaker can arrange the material so that it moves from the simplest to the most complex, the most familiar to the least familiar, the least important to the most important, or the most acceptable to the least acceptable.

Conclusion

The methods of concluding a speech were explained in detail in Chapter 8. However, certain concluding techniques are especially effective with informative speeches. For example, it may be helpful to restate the message and summarize its main points: "Today, we have seen that your grades can be improved if you select the correct location to study, learn how to determine the key points in your textbooks, and know how to prepare for objective examinations."

The most popular concluding technique is a *final summary* (or *reiteration*). Listeners tend to pay close attention when they sense the end of the speech is near. The final summary capitalizes on this heightened attention by reviewing the main ideas in the same order they were presented in the initial summary and in the body of the speech. Remember that the final summary should simply repeat the introduction and the main points of the body. If the introductory summary said that the audience would learn (1) how to prepare for an earthquake, (2) how to deal with the quake while it is going on, and (3) what to do once the quake is over, these three ideas should be repeated in the conclusion: "You should now know what to do before, during, and after an earthquake."

Sample Outline

Using the preceding discussion on the different components of informative speaking, we can now look at a sample outline to review the relationship among those parts.

Title: Who Pays?

General Purpose: To inform

Specific Purpose: To have the audience understand the major arguments for and against state aid to parochial schools.

Introduction

(Rhetorical Question)

I. How many of you realize that one of the crucial battles that raged during the founding of this country remains an unresolved issue today?

 A. The early colonists were determined to separate church and state.

 B. Yet compulsory school attendance laws meant that parents who desired private schools were forced to finance two separate institutions.

(Motivation Toward the Topic)

II. This highly emotional issue affects us today as much as it did over two hundred years ago.

 A. If the state were to pay tuition fees for private schools, millions of additional dollars would have to be found.

 1. Some of the money would come from our taxes.

 2. Money now being used to pay for public education would be reallocated to parochial schools.

 B. If the state were to support parochial schools, some say it would bring church and state closer together.

 C. Yet what about the people who believe that, under the First Amendment, we can educate a child in any way we deem appropriate?

 1. Is it not a denial of our freedom to be forced to pay dual taxation?

 2. What if you believe that our public schools are "Godless"?

(Speaker Qualification)

III. I am a political science major and have just completed my senior thesis on this topic.

 A. The paper focused on the specific issues involved in the separation of church and state.

 B. I plan to continue working on this project while attending graduate school.

(Preview)

IV. To better understand this important issue of state aid to parochial schools, I will examine the arguments frequently made in favor of tax support for these schools and then look at the arguments advanced by those who oppose such aid.

Core Statement: Opinion is strongly divided on the issue of state aid to parochial schools.

Body

I. Arguments that support tax aid for parochial schools are twofold.

    A. Denominational schools offer an important religious, spiritual, and ethical element not found in public schools.

        1. Only parochial schools are prepared to teach religious values.

        2. Public schools are "Godless."

    B. The right of parents to determine the education and religious instruction of their children is a fundamental one.

        1. Failure to provide public funds for denominational schools is a partial denial of that right.

        2. This denial may well make some families second-class citizens by depriving them of the full benefit from their taxes.

II. Arguments advanced by those who oppose tax support for parochial schools are threefold.

    A. The appropriation of public funds for denominational schools would be a major step toward breaking down the unique American policy of separation of church and state.

        1. It was part of an early colonial policy.

        2. It is an idea contained in the First Amendment to the Constitution.

    B. The organization of American public schools along denominational lines would make education a divisive rather than a unifying factor in our lives.

        1. Schools now teach a variety of opinions and views.

      2. Denominational schools would tend to teach religious dogma and one-dimensional attitudes.

    C. The present arrangements promote healthy growth among various religions.

Conclusion

(Summary)

I. Today, by looking at both sides of an important issue, we have gained some insight into the pros and cons of tax support for parochial schools.

    A. Those in favor of tax support suggest the following:

      1. Denominational schools can do a better job of teaching traditional values and ethics.

      2. It is unfair to deny a basic right to persons who select parochial schools.

    B. Those in opposition counter by saying the following:

      1. Granting funds for these schools would bring church and state closer together.

      2. Denominational education is divisive.

      3. The status quo is beneficial to both church and state.

II. In the final analysis, you must seek additional information before deciding how you feel about this important historical and religious problem.

This sample outline serves a dual purpose. First, it shows how to structure an informative speech. Second, it demonstrates how to prepare a balanced, objective presentation of a highly contentious topic. You should notice that the outline continually strives to present both sides of the controversy and never becomes an advocate for either side. The intent is to inform, and the final resolution is left to the listeners. In the next chapter, we will discuss the persuasive speech, which is designed to move the audience toward a specific opinion or action.

Chapter Summary

Speeches to inform are intended to increase an audience's knowledge of a selected subject. There are basically four types of informative speeches: (1) instructive, (2) descriptive, (3) explanatory, and (4) reports. When preparing a speech to inform, ensure that the specific purpose focuses on a worthwhile topic. When organizing an informative talk, prepare an introduction that arouses attention, creates interest, establishes speaker expertise, and previews the main points. The presentation's organizational sequence can be selected from a number of patterns: chronological, spatial, problem-solution, ascending-descending, causal, and topical. The most effective way to close an informative speech is to conclude with a summary.

Concepts and Questions

1. What is the primary objective of an informative speech?

2. What are the four basic types of informative presentations?

3. What should the introduction in the informative speech accomplish?

4. What devices help maintain audience interest?

5. Why is establishing your credibility important in informative speaking?

Activities and Exercises

1. Use one of your classes to analyze the professor's presentation in light of the material discussed in this chapter.

2. Select a technical topic and recount how you would explain some of the complicated aspects of the topic.

3. Select a single topic and write four different specific purposes. Each statement should reflect one of the following types of informative speeches.

   a. Instructive.

   b. Descriptive.

   c. Explanatory.

   d. Report. ✦

Chapter 10

Influencing Others With the Message

The Persuasive Speech

You are continually bombarded with messages urging you to take some course of action, adopt a particular perspective, or feel a certain way. Whether you are the sender or the receiver, persuasive messages are an integral part of your daily life. While you are watching TV, your favorite show is interrupted with commercial advertisements urging you to purchase products. In class, your professor uses persuasive appeals to motivate you to study for the forthcoming exam, or you may appeal for additional time on an assignment. In a commercial setting, you use persuasive cues, including nonverbal ones, to "sell yourself" during an interview. You use interpersonal appeals to convince friends to refrain from driving and drinking, to attend a new movie, or go to a certain restaurant. In short, whenever change is desired, persuasion is the main communicative means of achieving that change.

What Is Persuasion?

Previously, we saw that the objective of informative speaking is to increase the listener's understanding of a particular topic. Persuasive speaking is quite different. *In a* **persuasive speech** *the speaker, with conscious intent, seeks to modify or change the beliefs, attitudes, values, or behavior of his or her audience.* The key phrase in this definition is "conscious intent" in that the speaker knows *exactly* what is desired from the audience before the preparation and presentation process begins. This chapter examines some of the ways a persuasive speaker can ethically influence changes in the beliefs, attitudes, values, or behavior of listeners.

Types of Persuasive Presentations

Persuasive speeches can be classified according to the desired audience reaction. The three most general categories are speeches (1) to convince, (2) to actuate, and (3) to stimulate. While these types often overlap, knowing which type of speech will be given is the first step necessary in selecting arguments and appeals.

Speech to Convince

A presentation designed to get the audience to agree with the speaker's position is a speech to convince. A speaker might try to get the listeners to agree that there is too much violence on TV, or that the university "free speech mall" needs to set guidelines for how long a person can speak at that location. Talking about the need to overcome prejudice and embrace workforce diversity is also a speech to convince. Other examples of a speech to convince might be an attempt to persuade the audience that illegal immigrants' access to healthcare is seriously deficient or that tighter controls need to be instituted at our national borders to reduce the threat of terrorism. In each of these examples, the objective is to convince the audience of the validity of the speaker's claims.

Speech to Actuate

A presentation with the objective of stimulating audience action on a topic is a speech to actuate. Here, the emphasis is on motivating audience members to undertake a specific action. This activity element is evident when the audience is urged to participate in a weekend community service project, sign up for the campus International Student Center Friendship Program, vote for (or against) an increase in campus activity fees, or sign an organ donor card. In each of these instances, the audience is asked to do something, to engage in some type of activity.

Speech to Stimulate

A presentation with the goal of reinforcing, intensifying, or revitalizing listeners' existing attitudes or beliefs is a speech to stimulate. Such speeches can include efforts to arouse emotions, incite pride, or convey an inspirational message. Telling a class of incoming college freshman of the need to study hard or asking an audience to consider the plight of civilian causalities in Iraq and Afghanistan would be speeches that try to arouse basic beliefs. The goal in each of these instances is to remind the audience of a basic value they most likely already hold. Listeners are "stimulated" to once again think about that value. Occasions for stimulating speeches include sermons, motivational talks, and commencement addresses.

The Goals of Persuasive Speaking

In persuasive discourse, the speaker seeks to accomplish a specific, predetermined purpose by bringing about changes in the listeners' beliefs, attitudes, values, or behaviors. A persuasive speaker must be concerned with these four variables in order to achieve the intended persuasive objective. A speaker must ask this simple, but complex, question: "How must my audience change or modify their beliefs, attitudes, values, or behaviors if they are going to respond favorably to my recommendations?" To help answer this question, let us examine the key components of the four variables.

Beliefs

A **belief** is commonly defined as a personal conviction that a statement is true or that something exists. In a sense, it represents the framework of our reality. Such convictions can be based on factual proof or simply personal certainty. Individuals have beliefs about religion ("Muhammad was a messenger from Allah"), events ("U.S. intervention in Iraq was necessary"), other people ("Senator Smith would make an excellent president"), actions ("Promoting workforce diversity will increase profits"), and even themselves ("I am not ethnocentric"). Beliefs may be founded on direct experience, on the word of an authority, on input from a trusted friend, or on personal reasoning.

Beliefs are also influenced by culture. We are not born with our beliefs; they are learned, and culture is the teacher. Many Americans might acknowledge that the *New York Times* opinion page is a good place to learn about what they should believe. In the Islamic tradition, however, the belief is that the writings in the *Koran* are an infallible source of what to believe in. Our cultural background influences whether we trust the *Times*, the *Bible*, the *Koran*, the *Torah*, entrails from a goat, tea leaves, visions induced by peyote, or the Taoist *I Ching*. People raised in China, Cuba, or a rural West African village may believe that the means of production should belong to the state or to the people collectively. Conversely, someone raised in the United States, Canada, or Australia probably grew up believing that an individual "deserves what he or she earns" and would be reluctant to share profits.

Attitudes

*An **attitude** is a state of mind or an emotion toward a person or situation.* Attitudes reflect likes and dislikes toward persons, places, and things and are usually easier to change than beliefs are. You probably feel a certain way about talk shows, the characterization of women in rap videos, the requirement to take certain college classes, or the presentation style of one of your professors. Attitudes tend to guide people's responses to these and countless other subjects and orientations. These predispositions to behave one way or another are learned from family, the media, schools, religious affiliations, and the like. Culture writ large is a primary source.

Attitudes are important in persuasion because most persuasive efforts seek to either change or reinforce existing attitudes. A speaker must predict the audience's attitudes because the listeners' perspectives determine whether they will respond positively or negatively to the persuasive appeals. For example, if audience members have a positive attitude toward free market enterprise, they might easily support a legislative proposal to allow more foreign workers into the United States. In this case, your arguments are simple. However, if their opinion is that immigrant workers are taking jobs from U.S. citizens, the speaker will have to muster an entirely different set of arguments. Attitudes are so powerful that they can sway many decisions and actions.

Culture is an important factor in shaping and maintaining attitudes and causing them to vary from group to group across a wide array of topics. The popular feeling about gun control in Canada, Japan, and the United Kingdom is very different from that found in the United States. A Filipino-American's attitude toward the elderly may well be dissimilar to that of a Euro-American. Regardless of the subject, cultural attitudes play a definite role in audience message reception and must be considered.

Values

Values are another variable that influence what people may think or feel about a particular subject. Many of our most important beliefs and attitudes are grounded in our basic value system. **Values** *have* been called the evaluative components of beliefs and attitudes. Evaluative qualities include what is good or bad, right or wrong; what should or should not be; what is useful or useless; and what is appropriate or inappropriate. Values are hierarchically arranged, with some being more important than others. In short, values serve as a kind of "beacon" that helps people make choices and resolve conflicts.

The importance of values is that they form the foundation of most of our attitudes, beliefs, and actions. The value placed on a woman's right to choose influences an attitude toward abortion. Someone who places a high value on education may find it easier to support a plan to increase taxes for a new high school. A person who places a high priority on physical appearance might find it easier to refrain from spending time getting a tan if he or she learns that prolonged exposure to the sun dramatically increases the chance of skin cancer and gives the skin a leathery look as one grows older.

While each of us has our unique set of personal values, some values tend to be common to the majority of people in a culture. These **cultural values** are a product of the larger philosophical issues inherent in a particular culture. They define what is worthwhile for members of a culture to die for or protect, what frightens people, what subjects are proper for study or ridicule, and what types of circumstances lead to happiness or sadness. They include views of such topics as age, privacy, time, responsibility, change, equality, honesty, status, and work.

Behavior

Behavior *refers to an audience's observable activity*—what the audience members are or are not doing. Behavioral change represents the action component of persuasion. People are asked to do something that can be observed. Changes in behavior can take a person from action to inaction or the reverse; the change may involve an increase or a decrease in the intensity, duration, or magnitude of an action. For example, urging a close friend to discontinue binge drinking might produce one of these changes in behavior: your friend might drink more than ever out of defiance, might ignore your advice and continue to drink as usual, might reduce the number of binge drinking incidents, or might totally abstain from alcohol. Behavior changes are sometimes immediate (persuading people to sign a petition circulated after a talk), sometimes delayed (persuading people to avoid fast food restaurants the next time they eat out), and sometimes lasting (persuading people to stop drinking and driving). The acid test for the speech that stresses behavioral change is whether the audience is asked to act (behave) differently than they did before hearing the speech.

With this conceptual understanding of what constitutes, and the objective of, persuasive speaking, you are now ready to learn how to prepare a persuasive presentation.

Preparation of a persuasive speech involves the same steps used for an informative speech: (1) selecting a topic, (2) formulating a specific purpose, (3) analyzing the audience, (4) preparing supporting materials, (5) organizing the speech, and (6) practicing the presentation. Although all six of these steps have been previously discussed, the application of steps one through five to persuasion requires certain unique procedures.

Selecting the Topic

After determining that the objective of the presentation will be to persuade, your next step is to narrow the focus. Whether seeking to bring about changes in belief, attitude, value, or behavior, as a persuasive speaker you must formulate a specific proposition, one which describes the way you want your listeners to believe or act. Most propositions for persuasive speaking deal with questions related to facts, values, and/or policies, and a single speech might contain one, two, or all three of these questions.

Questions of Fact

When asserting that something actually exists, or is true, or did or did not occur, the issue involved is a question of fact. In these instances, the speaker's central point is termed a **proposition of fact**; he or she is attempting to prove or disprove the existence of something. The goal of the speaker is to persuade the audience that the proposition being asserted is true. The following are examples of propositions of fact:

- Better airport security screening is needed to prevent additional terrorist attacks.

- The Social Security System will run out of funds in the next 20 years.

- The affirmative action program is a failure.

- Prolonged exposure to TV and movie violence results in violent personal behavior.

- Population growth in the southwestern United States is creating unsustainable demands on local water supplies.

Questions of Value

If a speaker and a listener differ over the merit of a value judgment, the issue involved is a question of value, and the speaker's central point is termed a **proposition of value**. In other words, the speaker is placing an estimate of worth on something, alleging that it is good or bad, better or worse than something else, right or wrong, justified or unjustified. The following are examples of propositions of value:

- Abortion is immoral.

- The government has no right to make decisions about a woman's body.

- Prayer should be allowed in public schools.

- The separation of church and state must be maintained.

- Same sex marriage should be recognized.

- Same sex marriage is immoral.

Like propositions of fact, propositions of value may deal with matters in the past ("The United States mistreated American Indians"), present ("Minorities are stereotyped on most television programs"), or future ("Same sex marriage is a threat to traditional family values").

Questions of Policy

Differences between a speaker and a listener over the advisability of pursuing a specific course of action are **propositions of policy**. The speaker argues that something should or should not be done. Questions of policy ask for a specific action to be taken or for a new policy to be established. That policy or action can be personal

("Birth control pills should be available from the campus health center") or general ("The federal government should raise the tax rate on gasoline"). Here are some sample propositions of policy:

- The consumption of alcohol should be banned at Sunset Beach.

- Gasoline prices should be regulated.

- The state government should increase funding for higher education.

- The proposed student activity fee should not be used to fund athletics.

- The Internet should be strictly regulated to protect children from pornography.

It is not unusual for a speaker to include all three kinds of propositions (fact, value, and policy) within a single speech. For example, a speaker trying to win support for a proposed policy usually has to prove several propositions. Someone urging a change in the U.S. immigration policy might use the following:

- Something is wrong with the current immigration system— *proposition of fact:* "There are too many illegal aliens in the United States."

- The proposed plan will help solve the problem—*proposition of policy:* "A guest worker program needs to be enacted."

- The proposed policy is better than other proposals advanced— *proposition of value:* "We will gain control of our borders and reduce the exploitation of foreign workers."

Formulating a Specific Purpose

Once the topic has been selected it is time to decide on the statement of specific purpose—which indicates exactly what you want the audience to believe, feel, or do:

- For the audience to believe that gay marriage threatens traditional family values.

- For the audience to participate in a parade demanding the recognition of gay marriages.

- For the audience to feel a degree of sympathy for underprivileged third world orphans.

- For the audience to believe that all professional sports players should be tested for steroid drug use.

After formulating the specific purpose, audience analysis is the next step in a persuasive speech.

Analyzing the Audience

Although previously discussed, the importance of audience analysis in persuasive speaking requires a revisit to this critical step. Indeed, the major failures in persuasive speaking can probably be traced to an insufficient or inaccurate analysis of the individuals or group the speaker wishes to influence.

In analyzing listeners, speakers should try to answer the following questions: (1) What attitudes, beliefs, and values do they currently hold about the topic? (2) What has influenced them to take their current positions? (3) What is their attitude toward me as a spokesperson? Answers to these questions will provide a greater appreciation of the link between audience analysis and persuasive speaking.

There are many individual and group attitudes toward any topic. However, those attitudes will generally cluster along a continuum under the following headings: *apathetic, hostile, interested but undecided,* and *favorable.* It is important to try to determine which attitude is most representative of the audience and why they hold that position. Doing so will help in selecting the arguments and appeals that directly relate to the audience's beliefs, attitudes, and values. An analysis of the audience must also include an evaluation of their perception of you as the speaker. Because of its importance, speaker credibility in persuasive presentations is discussed in great detail later in the chapter. For now, just remember to include all dimensions of credibility early in the preparation stage.

Preparing Supporting Materials

The earliest theories of persuasion were formulated by the ancient Greeks. Aristotle's *Rhetoric*, which was written some 24 centuries ago, is still considered a definitive work on persuasion. In *Rhetoric*, Aristotle concluded that *to change the mind or behavior of other people, one must have a sound argument, appeal to their emotions, and be perceived as a highly credible source.* Contemporary research in the field of persuasion continues to support Aristotle's conclusions. Therefore, in this section, we explore (1) convincing arguments, (2) motivational appeals, and (3) personal credibility.

Convincing Arguments

The two key requirements for a rational argument are *reasoning* (i.e., how thoughts and material are organized) and *concrete evidence.* Most evidence falls into one of two categories: evidence of fact or evidence of opinion.

Evidence of Fact. Factual evidence is a crucial part of any speech to persuade and can be drawn from personal observations or external sources. Personal observation facts are used on a daily basis. For example, you might describe personal experiences in a previous class and tell others that the course had only two written assignments and a final examination. Factual evidence (e.g., examples, illustrations, and statistics) can also be drawn from outside sources such as newspapers, academic journals, census reports, scientific studies, and so on. Persuasive arguments need factual evidence if listeners are to believe the speaker's assertions and observations. For example, if you are trying to show the impact of moving technology jobs from the United States to other nations, the following facts could be used as support:

> According to current government estimates, U.S. technology jobs being shifted to India will reach 150,000 within the next three years and 2 million jobs will be relocated to off-shore (i.e., foreign) centers by 2014.

The effective persuasive speaker uses facts to help convince listeners that they should believe the validity of the assertion being advanced.

Evidence of Opinion. Opinion evidence has two sources: personal opinions based on one's own experience and the opinions of others who are recognized as experts. If, by reason of occupation or major field of study, you qualify as an expert—and if the audience recognizes those qualifications as adequate—you may use yourself as a source of opinion. By and large, however, student speakers are best served by relying on the testimony of a recognized authority. Consider the added credibility of a position on the global influence of information technology if the speaker offers the following evidence of opinion: "Frances Cairncross, an editor with *The Economist,* has reported that national and organizational cultural changes may have to occur before companies can benefit from information technology."

Motivational Appeals

People are complex and consumed with emotional and psychological feelings. The forces that motivate and impel them to act are multiple and complex—far too complex to be analyzed in a few pages of a textbook. Philosophers, pastors, and psychologists nevertheless seem to have agreed on a handful general forces that influence people's actions. These include:

1. *Self-preservation.* Safety devices, physical fitness courses, and life-prolonging medications are examples of goods and services that provide a partial answer to people's need to stay alive and enjoy physical well being. Construction workers who wear hard hats and buy shoes with steel-reinforced toes are acting out of a desire for self-preservation.

A familiar tactic in soliciting support for increased military spending is to use self-preservation as the appeal: "With the growing threat of small, radical nations acquiring nuclear weapons, we need to move quickly to develop a modern, effective strategic missile defense system." Self-preservation is also the obvious motive when politicians call for tax increases to fund additional police and fire fighting capabilities.

2. *Fear.* Much of our behavior is motivated by fear. We fear the loss of our money and possessions, loved ones, health, job, and in fact all those things we deem important. Speakers who tell us to wear seat belts, get flu shots, and eat healthy foods are appealing to our fear of the possible consequences that will occur if we ignore their assertions.

3. *Self-esteem.* At times, we will sacrifice personal safety, sublimate sexual desire, and disdain the acquisition of property if it means that our self-esteem can be increased. The desire to be "looked up to," to be well regarded by our peers or superiors, and to be perceived as responsible and reliable, is a powerful motivating force. It can show up in such diverse actions as donating a large sum to charity, enrolling in night school, skydiving, "standing up for your rights," or driving an expensive sports car. Extended to

groups, self-esteem takes the form of civic pride, a desire to be "number one," a wish to be the host city of the Winter Olympics, or an aspiration to have the world's finest medical research university.

4. *Personal enjoyment.* People's love of cars equipped with all the options, of exotic food and drink, of luxurious accommodations, of remote-controlled appliances, of all the so-called good things in life becomes a more dominant motive once their basic needs for food, clothing, and shelter have been met. People do not buy a mocha latte for its life-sustaining qualities but for its ability to bring pleasure to their taste buds. They do not buy a $60,000 SUV just to get from place to place but to satisfy their love of the good things. Items such as iPods, flat-screen TVs, hang gliders, and computer games are acquired primarily to satisfy a desire for personal enjoyment. A sales pitch detailing the pleasures of a Caribbean cruise would be a persuasive appeal to people's desire for personal enjoyment.

5. *Loyalty.* Whether their allegiance and loyalty is directed toward a country, state, community, or campus, people are all proud of their affiliations. A speaker who is aware of this devotion to country or club can effectively use it to motivate an audience. An example of using loyalty as a motive appeal would be telling a group of alumni, "Unless we get the money for the new library, our university will become a second-rate institution."

6. *Individualism.* Although a very Western trait, individualism is an effective motiving force. In the dominant American culture, individualism is the belief that the interest and welfare of the individual is paramount. It stresses individual initiative and encourages free expression. If speakers can link their central themes to these characteristics, they can greatly improve the chances of accomplishing their persuasive purposes. Recently, a speaker justified the need to spend more money on police protection by suggesting that when burglars enter a home illegally, they violate the owner's private domain. Conversely, for a predominantly collective oriented audience, the justification could have been that the potential for home burglaries represents a threat to the stability of the entire community.

7. *Altruism.* People like to think that they are compassionate and that most of their actions are not selfishly motivated. They make anonymous donations to charity, send CARE packages abroad, and volunteer to read to the blind. A successful persuasive speaker is well aware of altruism and uses this appeal when requesting help for victims as diverse as abandoned animals and neglected children.

Notice in the example that follows (on the subject of donating funds to UNICEF) how the speaker connects compassion to her topic:

> The little children huddle quietly in small groups, staring at you with vacant eyes. Their stomachs are swollen from malnutrition. They do not seem to notice the clouds of flies that hover around them, frequently landing on their hands and faces. The seasonal rains have left standing pools of water where malaria-carrying mosquitoes are now breeding. There are no schools or playgrounds. The children spend their days waiting in the oppressive heat, hoping that relief agency representatives will arrive with food, clothing, and tents for shelter. These are the children of interethnic conflict. They are the children that were forced to flee from their homes in the Darfur region of western Sudan, into the sprawling refugee camps along the border with Chad. Many of their parents were raped and massacred. The scene is absolutely heartbreaking because they are so small and their need is so great.

A speaker should keep some of the following ideas in mind when using motivational appeals:

1. *Try to consider using as many appropriate appeals as possible, because not all members of an audience are motivated by the same appeal.* Needs and wants differ from individual to individual and from culture to culture. For instance, if you are speaking about opposing the construction of a new airport near a residential area, the audience may consist of citizens who live in the affected area, others who live in the same city but not close to the affected area, and still others who are residents of other cities hundreds of miles away. Moreover, they might be of diverse ages, financial means, social classes, and value systems. With such a heterogeneous audience, it would be folly to rely on a single type of appeal. Although a fear appeal (threat to self-preservation) might stimulate those who live in the affected area, it would be far less applicable to those from another part of the city. They might be more motivated by an economic appeal (e.g., the high cost of acquiring residential/commercial properties). Pointing out to audience members who live in other cities that their personal enjoyment of the natural beauty of the area is threatened by the loss of open space or parks would also be appropriate.

2. *Always combine emotional appeals with logical appeals.* This blending allows an audience to see the wisdom of a proposal at the same time as they are "moved" by it. Notice in the following example, dealing with stricter drunk driving laws, how a motivational appeal (in the form of a factual illustration) is fused with statistics:

> The holiday season was special to nine-year-old Carla and her family. Carla's birthday was five days before Christmas, and her grandmother's birthday was Christmas Eve. The family was going to celebrate both birthdays and Christmas that night. So, for this young girl, as the family headed down the highway, a very special night was awaiting her. However, one thing went dreadfully wrong. On the way to the family gathering, a drunk driver, with two times the legal limit of alcohol in his blood, crashed into the side of the car where Carla's head was resting. The bright, cheerful, loving child was killed instantly. Carla would not get to open presents on Christmas morning with her family. In fact, like the other 2,000 people killed by alcohol-related crashes between Thanksgiving and New Year's Eve, Carla would never get to celebrate another Christmas. Instead, Christmas will always remain for Carla's family a tragic remembrance of the cruelty of drinking and driving.

3. *Whenever possible, use specific and personal examples when employing motive appeals.* It is easier to visualize a single case than an abstract number. Think about the hurt and impact you would feel if one of your best friends or a family member died of AIDS as compared to how you would respond to a statement that over 200,000 deaths have been reported from AIDS in the last 10 years. Motivational appeals should be personalized.

Speaker Credibility

Two speakers argue the same cause on separate occasions, using essentially the same lines of reasoning and similar evidence. However, the audiences tend to agree with one speaker, while the other fails to change any opinions. Why? Something about that one speaker inspires believability. What is the difference? Many words are used to describe this phenomenon—including "image," "charisma," "character," and "credibility." Regardless of the word used, the point is that often, despite the evidence cited and the motivation appeals employed, all efforts are wasted if the audience does not perceive the speaker in a positive manner. Character can influence the audience as much as content.

Credibility is generally what the audience thinks of the speaker and his or her causes. But what constitutes credibility? Aristotle maintained that if a listener perceived a speaker to have good character, good sense, and goodwill, the presented arguments were more apt to be believed. For Aristotle, an audience assigned speaker credibility based solely on the verbal message. Contemporary communication theorists, however, now consider the speaker's nonverbal behavior to be a factor in establishing credibility.

Also, they point out that credibility is partly a product of a speaker's established reputation. The theorists use terms such as (1) competence (being knowledgeable), (2) trustworthiness (having integrity), and (3) dynamism (displaying attractiveness) in discussing personal credibility.

These three components of credibility are examined more closely in the following paragraphs, which suggest some facets of speaker behavior to which Euro-American audiences respond favorably. However, people from other cultures or co-cultures may not use the same traits to judge credibility as members of the dominant American culture do.

Competence. Demonstrating competence takes a number of forms. For example, a speaker can manifest competence through intelligence and mastery of the subject. In general, conducting extensive research, using a variety of evidence, showing insight into the question, and using both logical reasoning and "common sense" enhance the speaker's credibility. Here are some specific things you can do to contribute to your perceived level of competence:

1. *Use proper language.* Nothing lowers credibility faster than a poor vocabulary, mispronunciation, or the misuse of language.

2. *Create clear and original visual aids.* Poorly constructed visual aids suggest a lack of interest in the topic and indicate poor preparation.

3. *Use credible sources and cite those sources.* The audience will often link the high-credibility source to your personal credibility.

4. *Start the speech on time.*

5. *Project an image of competence by appearing poised and relaxed.*

6. *Use a variety of forms of support.* The variety and quality of supporting evidence attests to the speaker's level of knowledge on the subject.

7. *Using good taste and humility, inform the audience of any personal experiences that qualify you as an 'expert' on the topic.* (If you are being introduced, the person providing the introduction should include your qualifications).

Trustworthiness. This characteristic is also referred to as integrity, honor, altruism, goodwill, or ethical character. Regardless of the label, an audience's perception of the speaker as a sincere, honest person is one of the most important aspects of successful public speaking. Some actions you can take to convey integrity include:

1. *Remember that moderation is usually equated with reasonableness.* Although intellectual enthusiasm and commitment are admirable traits, most people are fearful of extremism. People tend to be wary of someone who indulges in overstatement or unseemly emotional displays.

2. *Always employ tact.* Tact is the ability to deal with others without giving offense.

3. *Keep in mind that objectivity contributes to personal credibility.* Using material and sources that are fair and unbiased conveys a feeling of objectivity. Remember, perception is reality.

4. *Be sincere.* Sincerity is greatly admired in all cultures.

5. *Establish commonality with the audience.* People tend to trust speakers with whom they can identify. You need to convince the audience that you share some of their concerns, values, attitudes, and beliefs. If possible, bring out similarities and commonalities in backgrounds.

6. *Have the courage of your convictions.* Most audiences admire speakers who "stand by their convictions," even if the position they take is unpopular.

7. *Be honest.* Such things as acknowledging the existence of opposing views, not withholding contrary evidence, and ad-

mitting that there might be some legitimate drawbacks to
the proposal reflect honesty.

Dynamism. Dynamism is an abstract term encompassing such
things as a speaker's self-presentation and attractiveness. A dynamic speaker is energetic, enthusiastic, compassionate, strong, and
confident. Specific behaviors that contribute to a speaker's ability to
project a dynamic image include:

1. *Eye contact.* Effective "eye contact" allows you to "connect"
   with the audience.

2. *Personal appearance.* You should be dressed appropriately for
   the occasion. In most public-speaking situations, credibility
   is directly linked to a well-dressed and neatly groomed
   speaker.

3. *Facial expressions.* A smile is a powerful communication tool.

4. *Enthusiasm in voice and body.* If your outward expressions are
   passive, dull, indifferent, and listless, the audience might assume that you have little interest in them or the topic under
   discussion. Enthusiasm also tends to be contagious. If you
   feel good about yourself, you might stimulate similar feelings among the audience, producing a favorable disposition
   toward your topic.

5. *Relaxed demeanor.* A tense, nervous speaker is likely to be perceived as being ill prepared.

Organizing a Persuasive Speech

A disorganized presentation is guaranteed to be ineffective. To
avoid this problem, we will examine how to best organize a persuasive speech. More specifically, we will look at the principal functions
of the introduction, body, and conclusion. While these parts of a
speech have previously been described, the following discussion
shows how they specifically apply to a persuasive presentation.

Introduction

As we established earlier, the primary functions of an introduction are to gain the audience's attention and to prepare them for
what is to follow. In a persuasive speech, these two functions have
to be accomplished in a way that creates a climate of acceptance.

When asking an audience to change or alter a belief ("Run off pollution at local beaches is a serious problem for our city"), or to behave in a different manner ("You should avoid high-fat diets"), the speaker must establish audience rapport while simultaneously arousing their interest. It is also important to affirm your credibility early in the speech. If you are announcing the central point or core statement during the introduction, consider phrasing it in the form of a question. Compare these two ways of orienting an audience:

- Today, I would like to discuss with you the question, "Are our local water supplies safe from terrorism?"

- Today I will attempt to demonstrate that local water supplies are vulnerable to terrorist attack.

Which of the two statements has the strongest appeal to you? Experienced speakers have found that illustrations (hypothetical or factual), rhetorical questions, or startling statements are effective when opening a persuasive speech.

Body

The body of a persuasive speech contains the defense of the persuasive proposition. When defending a proposition of policy, you should present arguments to show the need for that policy and explain how your proposal will satisfy that need. When defending a proposition of fact or value, offer criteria to measure the truth of the fact or value judgment in question and then apply those criteria. Regardless of the type of persuasive speech you are giving, it is important to design a strategy that facilitates presenting the best case.

Conclusion

The conclusion of a persuasive speech should leave the audience with an attitude conducive to accomplishing your goal. For example, if your objective is to actuate, the audience should leave the presentation ready to engage in the desired action. If your goal is to convince, the audience should depart the presentation in agreement with your propositions.

Structuring the Persuasive Speech

Just as the objectives of an informative speech and a persuasive presentation are different, so is the organization. The need to move the audience to take a particular action or adopt a specific attitude requires more convincing than simply providing information. Over the years, several organizational patterns have proved effective for a persuasive speech. The following provides examples of two of most widely used organizational styles: the *problem-solution pattern* and the *motivated sequence*.

Problem-Solution Pattern

The problem-solution pattern is effective when you are attempting to persuade an audience to implement a specific policy. This is one of the simplest outline forms and is based on dividing the body of a speech into three parts. After an introduction to gain attention and orient the listeners, the speaker moves into the body of the speech, which is subdivided into sections that (1) present the problem area, (2) explain the solution to the problem, and (3) defend the solution. The speech concludes with an appeal for the appropriate belief or action. Here is an example of an outline for a speech structured around the problem-solution order:

Introduction

I. While driving home from work last Tuesday, I saw a Toyota SUV plow into a Ford pickup, which spun into a BMW sedan that ended up halfway underneath a garbage truck.

    A. I stopped my car and went over to help the injured people.

    B. One of those hurt in the accident was our classmate LaToya.

II. The location of that pileup was Grand and Main, an intersection that has experienced many similar accidents.

Core statement: A left-turn traffic light should be installed at the intersection of Grand and Main.

Body

Problem:

I. The intersection presents the worst traffic hazard in town.

Support:

    A. It is the scene of numerous collisions.

        1. (Evidence)

        2. (Evidence)

Support:

   B. It creates a bottleneck during morning and afternoon rush hours.

      1. (Evidence)

      2. (Evidence)

Cause:

II. The cause of this problem is the lack of a left-turn traffic light at the intersection.

Support:

   A. Cars attempting left turns from Grand onto westbound Main become targets of cars traveling southbound on Grand.

Support:

   B. Cars waiting to turn left produce a backup of homebound traffic on Grand.

Solution:

III. A left-turn traffic light would correct the existing problem.

Support:

   A. It would minimize collisions.

Support:

   B. It would speed up northbound traffic on Grand.

Defense:

IV. A left-turn traffic light would be practical to install.

Support:

   A. It would be practical from an engineering standpoint.

      1. (Evidence)

      2. (Evidence)

Support:

   B. It would be practical from a financial standpoint.

      1. (Evidence)

      2. (Evidence)

Defense:

V. A left-turn light would not present any disadvantages.

Support:

    A. It would not create any hazards.

Support:

    B. It would not be aesthetically unpleasing.

Defense:

VI. A left-turn light is the best solution to the problem.

Support:

    A. It would be less costly than an overpass.

Support:

    B. It would be more convenient than rerouting northbound traffic onto Cisco Avenue.

Conclusion

  I. I have attempted to demonstrate that a solution to this dangerous traffic condition does exist.

  II. You can help this proposal become a reality by signing the petition that I am about to circulate.

  III. Perhaps if we had had this light a week ago, LaToya might be in class today.

Monroe's Motivated Sequence

This organizational strategy is a variant of the problem-solution style and is useful for speeches that ask the audience to take a specific action. As the name suggests, the motivated sequence has a psychological orientation and attempts to move listeners through a succession of both logical and emotional steps. The five steps in the sequence (attention, need, satisfaction, visualization, action) are examined in the following skeleton outline.

General aim: To persuade.

Specific purpose: To convince the audience that severe punishment is needed to solve the rape problem.

(Step 1: Attention)

I. During today's class period, over 80 women will be raped in the United States.

    A. This means that approximately 700,000 adult women are raped each year

    B. Last year we had over 100 rapes reported in our city alone.

    C. Called by the American Medical Association the "silent violent epidemic," many rapes go unreported.

Transition: Let me begin by mentioning some of the effects of rape and then move to what we can do about this problem.

(Step 2: Need)

II. The problem of rape is very serious.

    A. Many victims develop a post-traumatic stress syndrome.

        1. Symptoms can include fear, humiliation, anger, flashbacks of the rape, and shock.

        2. A friend of mine who was raped was so traumatized that she had to withdraw from the university.

    B. Medical problems resulting from rape can include everything from acute injury to unwanted pregnancies.

    C. The consequences of being raped can be long lasting.

        1. Many rape victims avoid all contact with family members and friends.

        2. Many rape victims find it difficult to have any intimate sexual relationships long after the rape has occurred.

    D. According to the American Medical Association, very young people are often the target of rape.

        1. The AMA reports that 61 percent of all rape victims are under the age of 18.

        2. Some victims are as young as 11.

(Step 3: Satisfaction)

III. The serious problem of rape in our culture could be greatly reduced if the judicial system mandated harsher sentences.

A. A recent *Newsweek* article noted that only one in 100 rapists is sentenced to more than one year in prison.

B. Twenty-five percent of convicted rapists are put on probation and do not serve time in prison.

C. Many rapists are repeat offenders.

  1. According to Dianne Cruz, Director of the Crime Victims Association, "Rapists have such a high rate of recidivism that we often find many of them have been arrested for rape before."

D. What we all need to do is support legislation that mandates more severe punishments than what now exists.

  1. Rape convictions should carry a mandatory five-year jail sentence.

  2. A person convicted of rape for a second time should face a 20-year jail sentence.

(Step 4: Visualization)

IV. If we fail to act, rapists will continue to discover that the judicial system does not effectively stop them from performing their cruel acts.

A. After raping a 15-year-old girl, James Adams was sentenced to only six months.

B. His short jail term allowed him to rape again.

  1. He lured a 13-year-old girl into his house.

  2. He then tied her down with his belt and raped her.

(Step 5: Action)

V. Our legal system must reexamine the current approach it is taking toward rapists.

A. We must remove them from our society so they cannot repeat their callous acts on innocent women.

B. As you leave class today, remember the 80 who were raped while you and I were safe in this room.

C. Please consider writing your government representatives urging greater attention to this cancerous problem.

Persuasion and Culture

While culture is an important consideration in every aspect of public speaking, it is especially salient when dealing with persuasive appeals. As we will discuss, cultural variations also occur in argumentation, psychological appeals, and manifestations of speaker credibility.

Culture and Convincing Arguments

Cultural Variations in Evidence. In the West, public debate enjoys an especially long history. Many of the early democracies of Greece and Rome were built on the traditions of argumentation and persuasion. Even today, Western cultures (German, English, Euro-American) believe that the best methods for persuasion demand the use of sound arguments and the application of reliable evidence. People prefer concrete data. But people in some cultures (Latin American, Arab, American Indian) favor stories, allegories, analogies, and parables. Members of these cultures have long believed that stories are a powerful form of evidence. There are also cultural idiosyncrasies with regard to what constitutes a reliable source. In one culture, an authority is someone associated with religion, while in another the authority is the oldest person, and in yet another, the individual with the most education is the authority. In cultures that do not have a long tradition of a free and open press (Chinese, African, Russian), even the citing of so-called reliable sources does not have the impact it does with an audience composed of only Euro-Americans.

Quantity of Evidence Used. There are also differences in the amount of evidence that people from various cultures expect. Cultures that emphasize logic (Western European, Euro-American), and de-emphasize feelings and emotions, anticipate that a persuasive speaker will offer a great deal of evidence to support the claims. In cultures that show feelings and are more emotional (Latin, African, Arab), less evidence and more motive appeals might be the rule.

Cultural Variations in Reasoning. The mental processes of reasoning prevalent in a community are another major characteristic of culture that often influences the persuasive process. Western forms of lineal thinking and logical reasoning patterns assume a direct relationship between mental concepts and the concrete world of reality. This orientation places great stock in logic and rationality. Most Westerners believe that truth is "out there" and can be discovered by following scientific methods and engaging in logical, linear calculations. This Western form of linear thinking is in contrast with the Eastern view, best illustrated by Taoist, Buddhist, and Zen thought, which holds that cognitive reasoning works quite differently. Followers of these beliefs do not think that people are granted instant rationality. In fact, there is even a strong belief that intuition transcends the data of the senses. People who hold this view do not believe that one finds truth through active search, discussion, and applying Aristotelian modes of reasoning. On the contrary, one should patiently wait and if truth is to be known, it will make itself apparent.

Culture and Psychological Appeals

Cultures differ in both the number of emotional appeals considered appropriate and the content of those appeals. As just noted, some cultures rely on linear logic and "facts," while others are more comfortable focusing on relationships and emotions. Italians, Portuguese, Arabs, and Mexicans believe that sincere and emotional feelings transcend rigid syllogisms and tangible facts. Conversely, many people in the Euro-American culture believe that factual logic is the most persuasive method and that persuasion rooted only in emotional appeals should be avoided. This view often clashes with cultures that appreciate a speaker with a rhetorical flair.

When selecting specific motive appeals, knowledge of the audience's cultural composition is important. What appeals to one culture may not inspire another. Appeals that center on material possessions might be effective in one culture, but that same plea would not work with cultures that value a spiritual life over the acquisition of property. Some cultures value modesty (Arab) and would find sexually related appeals somewhat offensive. Even linking the message to fear should be carefully analyzed if an audience is culturally mixed. Some cultures tend to be apprehensive about the future and the uncertainty of life (Japanese, Greek, French), while others are not usually disconcerted by life's ambiguities (North American, Danish, Swedish, English). A speaker needs to learn as much as possible about the cultural characteristics of audience members when deciding if motivation appeals should be used and how to make the appeals compelling and forceful.

Culture and Personal Credibility

The chapter's earlier discussion of credibility was based solely on what influences a Euro-American audience. Listeners from other cultures prize different types of behavior. The people of Japan, China, and other East Asian cultures tend to look favorably on a speaker who uses few words, since such behavior suggests reflectivity. There is a Japanese proverb that says, "He who speaks has no knowledge and he who has knowledge does not speak." The Chinese have a saying, "Fear the dog that is not barking." Most Asian listeners are leery of speakers who are wordy, direct, impulsive, or assertive. Although American listeners regard self-disclosure favorably, German and Japanese audiences view it as a breach of good taste. Israeli, Mexican, and Greek cultures expect speakers to be very animated and emotional in their visual and vocal mannerisms. To be otherwise would raise suspicion about the speaker's lack of conviction. Since Arab cultures deem it important for speakers to use a great deal of embellishment in their language, an effective multicultural speaker addressing an Arab audience would probably make greater use of metaphors and similes than when addressing a Euro-American audience. In many cultures (Latin American, Asian, German), a speaker's status and reputation greatly promotes the development of credibility.

Persuasion and Ethics

Never forget the link between communication and ethical behavior. Your actions produce serious results—they change the thinking and behavior of other people. As a West African proverb notes, "If it rains on the mountaintop, it is the valley below that gets flooded." Because change is at the very core of persuasion, we suggest six questions to help you determine whether you are being an ethical speaker:

1. Who will benefit from my persuasive speech?

2. Is inflammatory language being used to help accomplish my goal?

3. Are fear appeals being misused?

4. What is the cultural composition of the audience?

5. Have I been ethical in gathering information?

6. Would I like to be treated in the same manner I am going to treat the audience?

Chapter Summary

Persuasion is the process of convincing listeners to voluntarily change their beliefs, attitudes, values, and behavior. Successful persuasion rests on a thorough knowledge of the audience and its attitudes toward the speech topic, the speech purpose, and the speaker. The objects of change are the listeners' learned predispositions, convictions, and manifest behavior—particularly with respect to issues of policy, fact, and value. A speaker's position should rest on an awareness of the audience's perception of the subject.

According to Western rhetorical tradition and modern social psychology, the means of persuasion lie in logical appeals, psychological appeals, and the listeners' perception of the speaker's personal credibility. The components of logical persuasion are evidence and reasoning. Evidence should come from an authoritative source and should be recent, capable of corroboration, and objectively presented.

Persuasion through psychological appeals is traditionally thought to involve the use of motivation and suggestion. The needs and wants to which the speaker may link the message include self-preservation, fear, self-esteem, personal enjoyment, loyalty, individualism, and altruism. Suggestion is the arousal of a response by indirect means. It may operate through channels external to the speaker, the speaker's delivery, or the verbal message. Persuasion through personal credibility is also possible when a speaker manifests the appropriate traits.

Although a persuasive speech can be organized in a variety of ways, certain methods seem to enjoy the greatest popularity. The problem-solution order and the motivated sequence are particularly appropriate for developing propositions of policy. A successful persuasive speaker understands the role of culture in persuasion. Culture will influence the arguments used, the selection of motivational appeals, and the way the audience perceives credibility. A final consideration is the ethical ramifications of appealing to an audience to change their belief systems or the way they behave.

Concepts and Questions

1. Explain the differences between beliefs, attitudes, values, and behaviors.

2. Why is audience analysis important when preparing a persuasive speech? What are some of the things that should be considered?

3. What are the major components of personal credibility?

4. What are the two most popular forms of organizing a persuasive speech, and how do they differ?

5. What are some considerations when presenting a persuasive presentation to a multicultural audience?

Activities and Exercises

1. List five specific ways to establish speaker credibility with an audience.

2. Write three specific purposes for a persuasive speech. Use propositions of fact, value, and policy.

3. Write a short essay that reflects your personal views on the role of ethics in persuasive speaking.

4. Listen to a talk radio program or a TV panel discussion and analyze how the people calling into the program do or do not use logical arguments and motivational appeals. ✦

Chapter 11

The Medium of the Message

Language and Communication Ethics

Language is one of the most important aspects of human interaction. Words allow us to express ideas, share feelings, and make inquiries. In accomplishing these communicative tasks, we continually make choices as to what words to use. In the public speaking arena, understanding how language works enables a speaker to make informed decisions when deciding on which words will help accomplish desired goals. For example, the listeners' background and culture influence the meaning they attach to words. An awareness of this reality allows a speaker to select words that are culturally appropriate, that are commensurate with the listeners' experiences, and that improve audience understanding.

This chapter discusses two principal communication topics, language and ethics. The first part on language talks about making the proper choices in order to match words with objectives. We discuss some general characteristics of language and explore techniques on how to use language in order to become an effective speaker. Finally, we offer advice on how to improve language usage.

In the chapter's second part, we examine an important but frequently overlooked subject, communication ethics. While communication has always been a key factor in humankind's development, it is a focal point in this age of information. This heightened importance has created a greater need to consider how we can communicate ethically. To help you understand your obligations, we will explore the responsibilities of both the speaker and the listener. We conclude the chapter with a discussion of the importance of listening.

Understanding How Language Works

What is language? One way to view **language** is as an organized system of symbols, both verbal and nonverbal, used in a common, uniform way to communicate thoughts and feelings. **Words** are the symbols used in verbal language, just as gestures, movements, and facial expressions are the symbols of nonverbal language.

Words Are Only Symbols

Succinctly, words are symbols used as substitutes for the "the real things." You cannot eat the word "apple" or drive the word "car." Words are abstractions used to represent those things. It is important to remember that there is no required or consistent relationship between a word and the thing it symbolizes. In reality, words are merely sounds, marks on paper, or symbols on a computer screen used to express what is in our heads. In short, words are arbitrary symbols. People who share the same culture and language have simply agreed that a certain sound or combination of sounds stands for a given thing, concept, or experience. In the English language, we have agreed that the word "horse" refers to a large four legged animal used for work and pleasure. But the Japanese have elected to use the word *uma* to represent horse, the French chose *cheval*, Spanish speakers selected *caballo*, Indonesians decided on *kuda*, and Swahili speakers picked *farasi*.

In short, words have no meaning in themselves; they only indicate what people think they mean. Words are the tools used when attempting to share reality, but because they are merely symbols they can hinder as well as assist. This awareness should guide your selection of the words in all communication events.

Words and Their Meanings Are Learned

Not only are words symbols, but the symbols, and the meanings they produce, are learned. Simply put, our meaning for a word is determined by our experiences with that word. Stated differently, the meaning we attach to a word is an outgrowth of the feeling, subject, event, or other thing we have *learned* to associate with that word. Growing up, most of us asked our parents, "What does that word mean?" However, in most instances children learn thousands of words simply through exposure. Because people often have dissimilar experiences, they also have different words and meanings for those experiences. To most of us, for example, the word "dog" probably carries a meaning of a domesticated pet that is often treated like a member of the family. Likewise, the word "horse" can suggest an animal that is used for pleasure or work. In other parts of the world, however, both "dog" and "horse" can elicit a very different image and definition. In parts of Asia, dogs are considered to be food, and in France and Japan, horsemeat is a delicacy. Thus, different personal and cultural experiences produce different definitions. It is important to remember that what is true with the simple examples of "dog" and "horse" applies to ideas and concepts that are much more involved. Think for a moment of how people from different backgrounds and experiences might variously define words and expressions such as "abortion," "AIDS," "affirmative action," "sexual harassment," "free choice," and even "democracy."

Words Have Many Uses

Often, we unconsciously assume that a word has a single meaning. In fact, the 2,000 most frequently used English words have approximately 14,000 different meanings. In everyone's vocabulary, there are countless words with multiple meanings and uses. For instance, the word "lap" can represent the distance around a track, a portion of one's anatomy, the drinking method of a cat or dog, or the sound of water washing gently against the side of a boat. A quick glance at any page of the dictionary will yield numerous words with multiple meanings.

The multiple meanings of the word "lap" are rather simple and uncontroversial. However, consider what can happen when a word or phrase has greater complexity or is contentious, such as "obscene," "gay," "liberal," "conservative," "pro choice," "right to life," or "family values." There is indeed more than one meaning and interpretation for each of these.

The addition of the cultural variable can bring still more confusion and ambiguity to the meaning of words. How would you express a meaning for "hamburger," "laptop computer," "affirmative action," "cellular phone," or "car jacking" to someone from a culture that does not have these experiences or expressions as part of its working vocabulary? As an example, try and remember the first time you heard the word "sushi," "croissant," "latte," or "taco."

Words Evoke Denotative and Connotative Meanings

Because meanings exist only in the mind, and not in the actual object, thing, or concept being described, people often hold different meanings for the same word. Meanings are also affected by the denotative and connotative aspects of words.

Denotative Meaning. The **denotative meaning** of a word is the one that society has sanctioned as the "official" or literal meaning, the meaning most often found in the dictionary. Denotative meanings are somewhat impartial and neutral, and seldom contain emotional overtones. There can be general agreement as to what represents a car, tree, chair, table, and the like. As previously mentioned, however, the dictionary may furnish several "official" meanings for a particular word. For example, "land" is variously defined as the solid portion of the earth's surface, as a country or nation, as a piece of real estate, as the act of catching a quarry such as a fish, as acquiring something, such as a job, or as the arrival of an airplane at a destination.

Dictionary definitions are usually phrased in nonjudgmental language. They tend to be factual and concrete. These denotative meanings normally cause public speakers little trouble. It is in the second category of meaning, connotative, where problems arise.

Connotative Meaning. **Connotative meaning** is the private, emotional meaning that a word evokes in the individual. It is the meaning that reflects your personal experiences and feelings with the thing or event the word represents. The connotations a word has for you are more likely to determine your response than the denotations. The word "taco" may conjure up images of a sunny beach and a nice meal enjoyed during a Spring Break trip to Mexico. On the other hand, it might bring to mind the unpleasant consequences of gastric distress suffered as a result of the meal.

Because connotations are more subtle and varied than denotations, they often cause confusion in intercultural transactions. Words such as "love," "hate," and "democracy" have a great number of connotations. For example, in the United States you can "love" good food, your mate, your parents, and your country. The word "love" is the same in each instance, but the connotations are quite different. For someone not from the United States, understanding the subtlety of these differences requires a high level of cultural awareness, which usually takes time to develop.

In an intercultural situation, a seemingly ordinary word can have powerful connotative meanings. Imagine your response to the word "tattoo" if you were raised with the understanding that normally only gangsters have tattoos, as is the case in Japan. However, if raised in the United States, where tattoos are common and socially accepted, your connotative meaning for the word would probably be positive.

Language and Intercultural Communication

A major theme of this book is that public speakers often find themselves addressing multicultural audiences. Thus, it is important to understand the influence of language when speaking to a culturally diverse group of people. Here are a few language variables that need to be considered.

Idioms

Confusion can easily arise when addressing people who are not completely familiar with the speaker's language, and the confusion is often compounded by the use of idioms. By definition, **idioms** do not lend themselves to literal translation. Try to imagine how people who use English as a second language would interpret the following expressions:

- "To be successful, you need an effective game plan."
- "You have to sell yourself."
- "The two negotiators did not seem to be on the same page."
- "They began the debate with two strikes against them."
- "We need to be careful that the tail does not wag the dog."

These examples illustrate the need to be aware that words carry multiple meanings and that some are tied directly to culture.

Ambiguity

Ambiguous language can be another source of difficulty when addressing individuals who are not native English speakers. When a word or statement is **ambiguous**, the meaning can be unclear or have multiple interpretations. When reading the following examples, imagine that English is your second language, and that you are trying to decode what is said by giving meaning to each word:

- The only thing holding up this bridge is red tape.

- Our local hospital is being sued by seven foot doctors.

- The lead painter was the first to arrive.

- The new program has cut high school dropouts in half.

- The stolen painting was found by the tree.

- Mating of the panda has failed—the veterinarian will take over.

Although these examples are humorous, they clearly demonstrate potential problems arising from the use of ambiguous language in intercultural communication.

Directness and Indirectness

Cultures are often distinguished by how they use language. One major cultural difference is in the use of direct and indirect language style.

Direct. Most of us are familiar with the direct style of language because it is the type most common in the United States. Directness is characterized by bluntness, explicit expressions, specific words, and a desire to be exact. The desire to be honest, accurate, and logical is of greater importance than maintaining amiable interpersonal relationships.

Indirect. Indirect language is found in many collectivistic cultures and especially in Northeast Asian nations. The indirect language style is characterized by vagueness and ambiguity, quite the opposite of direct language. Collectivistic cultures value the indirect language style because it lessens the potential for conflict and facilitates harmonious relationships. For instance, the Japanese try to avoid using the word "no" whenever possible, because "no" is considered too blunt and harsh. Instead, they may say something like, "That is interesting" or "Let me think about that." The desire for harmonious relations carries over into many of the Asian-American co-cultures—e.g., Filipino-American, Vietnamese-American, Korean-American, and Chinese-American—and produces an indirect communication style (Gudykunst 2001).

Eloquence

Some cultures, such as the Arabic speaking societies, emphasize rhetorical eloquence, while others, such as Euro-Americans, do not. Among Arabs, the ability to speak eloquently is a highly valued trait, reflected in their florid style. For instance, an Arabic speaker will often use embellishment, analogies and similes, repetition, and extended illustrations. The Greek culture also prizes the ability to speak eloquently. Drawing on their long tradition of rhetorical oratory techniques, the Greeks use a variety of key sayings and proverbs to express many feelings and ideas.

Formality

Some cultures, such as the German and English, place considerable importance on the use of formal language. When addressing an audience that embraces formality, speakers should not use slang, colloquialisms, jargon, and other types of casual language. If a culture values simplicity in the use of language (Japanese, Chinese, Korean), overstatement should be avoided. If rhetorical artistry is respected (Arab, Greek, and Mexican), a grander and more commanding style of address should be used. A requirement for every speaking occasion is a careful assessment of the audience, coupled with common sense and appropriateness.

The obvious question is what to do when encountering a multicultural audience. As we discussed earlier, there has been very little research in this area. Along with the suggestions offered in Chapter 7, we recommend you try to self-monitor your style and adjust to your perceptions of the audience's reaction as you make the presentation.

Speakers sometimes attempt to adapt their language to reflect another cultural style. But great care should be taken in this effort. For example, when speaking among themselves, many African Americans use Black English, or Ebonics, a recognized language form derived by overlaying English words with the grammar rules brought by slaves from West African languages. It would be foolish, embarrassing, and tactless, however, if a Euro-American speaker tried to adapt to an African-American audience by using Ebonics. The same is true of a middle-aged person who thinks he or she is being inspirational by using the vernacular of a high school student. Think about how you feel when your parents use this type of language.

Characteristics of Effective Style

With knowledge of how words work, we are now ready to examine their effective use. Style indicates how someone selects words and strings them together. Style also refers to how those words fit the audience and occasion. Saying the right thing, in the right way, at the right time is not an easy task. The following discussion is intended to help you develop an effective speaking style.

Effective Style Is Clear

Our discussion about the problems associated with language illustrates why clarity is considered the most important quality of good style. Audience members must be able to immediately understand the intended meaning of your words. It is impractical to think they can consult a dictionary during the presentation. Fortunately, there are a variety of ways a speaker can ensure a clear message.

Oral Style Promotes Clarity. Some specific ways oral style can promote clarity include the following:

1. *Posing rhetorical questions.* Rhetorical questions are intended to mentally stimulate the audience and provide an excellent means of arousing attention. When phrased correctly, they can relate the material directly to the audience. Rhetorical questions force listeners to become mentally involved in the speech. When speaking on the subject of multicultural education, a good rhetorical question would be, "What percentage of our children entering elementary school speak English as a second language?" This question brings the audience into the communication process by offering language that is concise, compact, and clear.

2. *Using repetition.* An effective oral style places greater reliance on repetition than a written style does. In written communication, the reader usually proceeds at his or her own speed; a page or paragraph can be reread to acquire understanding before moving on. In public address, however, the speaker determines the pace at which the "page is turned." Therefore, the use of repetition allows the speaker to increase the audience's opportunity to understand what is being said. Suppose you had just made an important point about the religious affiliations of Arab-Americans. You could further

emphasize and clarify the point by saying: "We have just seen the statistics on Arab-American religious affiliations. These figures clearly show that the majority of Arab-Americans are not Muslims" (Arab American Institute Foundation, 2002). Repetition helps increase understanding and reminds listeners what is considered important.

3. *Incorporating personal pronouns.* Talking directly to audience members enhances intimacy. A speaker can "connect" with the audience by using pronouns, such as "you," "we," "us," "our," and "I." Think about the impact of the following two sentences:

   • Before traveling to another country, *everyone* needs to learn some of the language and cultural habits.

   • Before traveling to another country, *you* need to learn some of the language and cultural habits.

The material can be further personalized by using the names of specific audience members: "Jorge was telling me just the other day about his friend Marta, who took a two-week introductory German course before visiting Berlin and Munich to attend two World Cup soccer games."

Natural Language Enhances Clarity. Whenever possible, use one word instead of two, a word with a clear meaning, and one sentence instead of two. Which is the clearer word in each of the following pairs?

Prevarication or lie?	Ennui or boredom?
Risible or laughable?	Sanguine or optimistic?
Betrothal or engagement?	Edifice or building?
Recapitulate or summarize?	Denouement or end?
Eschew or avoid?	Commence or begin?

Simpler words generally increase understanding and reduce ambiguity, especially for a multicultural audience.

Specific Language Promotes Clarity. A speaker who uses names, dates, places, and other details offers listeners a much clearer mental picture of what is being discussed. For example, "Lam and Freda went to a Navaho Nation powwow in Gallup, New Mexico, last summer" is certainly more specific than "They attended an American Indian cultural event last year." Being specific provides listeners a reasonably clear indication of what transpired. In many instances, only a word or two can make the difference between being vague and being clear. Think about how much more apparent the meaning is if you say, "during Spring Break" instead of "sometime this semester."

The following general and specific comparisons demonstrate how a more specific word helps a speaker produce a clearer meaning:

Table 11.1 *General Versus Specific Terms*	
General	**Specific**
animal	dog, horse, elephant, camel, cat
vehicle	car, bike, coach, motorcycle
worker	plumber, painter, carpenter, mason
Asian	Chinese, Japanese, Korean, Vietnamese
Asian American	Vietnamese American, Korean American, Thai American
Middle East	Jordan, Saudi Arabia, Iraq, Qatar
Europe	England, Germany, France, Poland
sports	baseball, basketball, football, soccer, sumo
vegetables	carrots, broccoli, green beans, yellow squash
exercise	walking, swimming, running
doctor	surgeon, pediatrician, urologist

The specific and concrete examples in the right-hand column clarify the discussion for the audience. It is easier to visualize a dog being abused than an animal being mistreated.

Effective Style Is Grammatically Correct

Using correct grammar is a requirement for keeping the audience's attention focused on the speech topic and maintaining speaker credibility. Incorrect grammar is a distraction, turns the listeners' attention to the erroneous expressions, and erodes the speaker's credibility. For these reasons, an effective speaker must avoid errors in syntax and grammar. Grammatical errors can also confuse audience members. Even though somewhat exaggerated, think about how distracting the following grammatically incorrect statements can be:

- I had wrote this petition a long time ago.

- There wasn't no easy way out.

- Me and my friend are going to the show.

- I think he done it.

- If we do not put a new light at that corner of Main and Second, someone will be hurt bad.

- Me and my group will not back this plan.

- It was, like, so hot that afternoon.

Effective Style Is Vivid

As important as clarity and grammatical correctness are, they may not be sufficient to hold audience attention, maintain interest, and create a favorable impression. Effective style also relies on the assistance of a third quality—vividness. To achieve vividness, successful speakers have relied on two fundamental methods: (1) imagery and (2) figures of speech. The following discussion demonstrates how each method can make ideas come alive and linger in the listener's mind.

Imagery Promotes Vividness. When a speaker uses imagery, listeners are asked to visualize a past event or to imagine a new situation that is being described. The objective is to have the audience vicariously experience the sensation being depicted. Imagery takes forms that correspond to the human senses. Language allows speakers to evoke sensations of sight, sound, smell, taste, and touch. Consider the various senses aroused by the following descriptions:

1. As I entered the small but noisy Irish pub, the acrid smell of tobacco assaulted my nose. As I pushed my way to the crowded bar, my eyes began to water, and I noticed the pale, blue cloud of smoke than hung lazily above everyone's head.

2. Riding a Tokyo subway during the morning rush hour can be quite an experience. So many people are crowded into each car that you are unable to move your hands from your side, and as the subway speeds through the underground tunnel, the crowd involuntary sways from side to side in seemingly synchronized unison.

In some instances, even a single word can make the speaker's point more vivid, colorful, and lively as in Table 11.2.

Table 11.2 Finding More Colorful Terms	
Standard	**Colorful**
horse	mount, nag, equine, stallion, bronco, filly
hot	scorching, torrid, blazing
walk	stroll, plod, shuffle, slink, trod
violent	turbulent, raging, explosive
cheap	frugal, scrimping, miserly, penny-pincher
poor	destitute, impoverished, insolvent
small	diminutive, paltry, scanty, tiny
loud	animated, deafening, booming, reverberating
silent	hushed, muted, quite

The composition of the audience and the context will influence which words and phrases are more appropriate. Regardless of these factors, however, the speaker's language should not be dull, mundane, or inanimate. At the same time, however, simplicity must be balanced with vividness.

Figures of Speech Promote Vividness. Figures of speech impart vividness to language and elevate the quality of the speaking style. Moreover, figures of speech can greatly increase a speech's vigor, clarity, and beauty, while adding to speaker credibility. Among the most popular figures of speech are metaphor, personification, hyperbole, climax, rhetorical questions and alliteration. We offer a brief discussion of each.

1. *Metaphor.* A **metaphor** is a comparison of dissimilar things that enable a speaker to say a great deal with very few words. The comparison is implied and built into a metaphor so the words "like" or "as" can be omitted. Abraham Lincoln, discussing the danger of two Americas, used the metaphor, "A house divided against itself cannot stand." A speaker talking about terrorism could incorporate a metaphor by saying, "The terrorist threat gave birth to increased airport security measures." In both examples, a figurative comparison suggests two dissimilar things are alike.

2. *Personification.* **Personification** is a figure of speech in which life and personality traits are attributed to inanimate objects or abstract ideas. The following are examples of this type figure of speech:

- That piece of cake was begging me to come and taste it.

- The problem has been with us so long that it is a member of the family.

- Even the stately faces on Mt. Rushmore looked a little sad after the 9/11 attacks.

3. *Hyperbole.* Based on exaggeration, **hyperbole** is a figure of speech that magnifies objects beyond their natural boundaries in order to make them more impressive and more vivid. Some examples are:

- It took Susan so long to enroll in the required classes that she and her daughter were in the same graduation class.

- There was so much hot air coming from those politicians that I thought the snow on the roof would melt.

- The music at the Los Angeles concert was so loud that the mayor of San Francisco called to complain.

4. *Climax.* Climax is a figure of speech that presents a series of thoughts or statements arranged in order of increasing importance. The building effect of climax gives impact to the statement:

The first fee increase caused me to take a part-time job. With the second raise, I had to find full-time employment in order to stay in school. With the latest charges, I am forced to leave school and abandon my education.

5. *Rhetorical questions.* Rhetorical questions are queries intended to produce a mental response among audience members. When using a rhetorical question as a figure of speech, it is often effective to ask a series of questions. Notice the verbal impact in the following example:

> Do you believe you are receiving the best education possible? Ask yourself these questions: How crowded are my classes? Do my professors know my name? Am I being challenged to do my best work? Are all my grades determined by multiple choice exams?

6. *Alliteration.* An alliteration is the repetition of a sound or a similar sound at the beginning of words. Alliterations can be used to add interest to the point being made. Notice the vividness in the following examples:

- The development project was doomed to fail. It was too costly, too complex, and too chaotic.

- This law is important for our community. We must persuade, prod, and push our legislature to adopt the proposal.

Effective Style Is Appropriate

Adaptability is an important characteristic of a successful speaker. Moving from one communication context to another necessitates an adjustment in style to meet the unique demands of each encounter. The style must be geared to the specific audience and the occasion.

Appropriate to the Audience. Language is an especially critical aspect of adapting to the audience. Recall how you change your words when moving between different audiences. In a professor's office to seek assistance or advice, your word selection is more precise and formal than when chatting with a group of friends at a coffee shop. As another illustration, consider the language you use with your friends compared to that used when talking with your parents or grandparents. Using language inappropriate for the audience will only defeat a speaker's objective.

Appropriate to the Occasion. The speaking occasion, or context, is an important determinant of what constitutes appropriate style. At the coffee house with friends, the language will normally be casual and relaxed. A college commencement address demands a more serious tone. A commencement speaker might say, "May the doors of learning, now opening to you and your fellow students, remain wide for the future generations of this great state," but, in a small group, that same statement could be perceived as pompous and out of place. Additionally, in public speaking, slang is seldom appropriate and obscenities should never be used.

Ethics and Language

There is also an ethical component of language usage. The words we use and the actions we take have an influence on other people. Our messages create change. Therefore, it is incumbent that some ethical guidelines be followed.

1. *Be accurate.* When presenting facts or describing a scene, use language that correctly and carefully represents reality. Language should properly present the facts.

2. *Be aware of the emotional impact.* Knowing the emotional impact that some words can have on an audience can help in avoiding language that touches the passions of the listeners in an unethical manner. This is not to suggest that animated and passionate language be totally avoided, but rather that when employing a style to arouse the emotions, do so in a way that does not exaggerate or falsely embellish the point being made. Overstated appeals to fear are an example of language use that is unethical.

3. *Avoid hateful words.* Hateful language is unethical! Words that are racist, that are sexist, or that speak maliciously of a person or group of people are examples of hateful language. An effective presentation should be forceful, honest, and free of hatred.

4. *Be sensitive to the audience.* It is insensitive not to respect the wishes of your culturally diverse audience if, as a group, they prefer words such as "Asian" to "Oriental," "gay" to "homosexual," "African American" to "black," and "disabled" to "handicapped." A speaker should also avoid language that tends to belittle others on the basis of gender or age.

Improving Language Habits

Although language habits and vocabulary are developed early in life, they are constantly open to improvement. However, improvement requires more than memorizing a few rules or formulas. It demands practice and hard work over a period of time. Language skills can be increased by the following activities:

1. Learn to use a dictionary and a book of synonyms. Both are available online and are an integral part of word-processing programs (e.g., Word, WordPerfect)

2. Be alert to new words when listening, writing, and reading. Learn their meanings and try to use them in conversation.

3. Be sensitive to the difference between oral style and written style. Language generated for speaking is somewhat different from written language.

Ethical Responsibilities of Communication

The topic of ethics is much discussed in contemporary society. Television, websites, and newspapers have been filled with reports on ethics. Events such as the collapse of Enron, the discovery of fraudulent news reporting, and cases of political corruption have made ethics a concern for everyone. However, the many media stories consistently forget to remind us just exactly what ethics are. Simply stated, **ethics** are the judgments we make every day concerning the degrees of rightness and wrongness and of virtue and vice. Ethics are the standards we employ to judge human behavior—our own and that of other people. In communication, ethics were important as early as the sixth century B.C., when Confucius wrote, "If language be not in accordance with the truth of things, affairs cannot be carried on to success." Nowhere is the notion of truth more profound than in the public-speaking arena. When you assume the role of the "speaker," you are asking other people to believe you, to trust you, and to adopt your recommendations. These are indeed ethical issues.

Ethics and Public Speaking

For centuries, the power of speech to influence people has raised weighty considerations. In *The Rhetoric*, Aristotle asserted that while the art of persuasion (changing behavior) is good in and of itself, it has the potential to be used to achieve either good or bad objectives, depending on the speaker's intent. The ability to change behavior through persuasive speech is so potent that a malicious person may use it to induce an audience to act unwisely or unjustly, as was done by Adolph Hitler in the 1930s and Saddam Hussein in the 1990s. In contrast, ethical persuasive speaking can produce great good, as demonstrated by Mahatma Gandhi, the Indian nationalist, motivating an entire nation to engage in nonviolent action in the 1930s, and Martin Luther King, Jr.'s appeals for civil disobedience and national equality in the 1960s.

Because communication is such a powerful instrument, the ethical implications of our messages must be considered. We will examine ethical responsibilities of the sender and of the receiver and the role of culture in determining ethical behavior.

The Sender's Responsibilities

Any misdeed or harm resulting from persuasive communication is a direct product of the people involved, not the processes of communication. The devices and means used by speakers are their own responsibility. Accordingly, the following questions should be considered each time a communication act is initiated.

1. *Why am I giving this speech?* An ethical speaker begins by examining the motives for the intended speech. Constantly asking yourself whether the purpose is responsible, reasonable, and honorable allows an evaluation of the speech's content and intent. Being conscious of this responsibility is an encouragement to ensure that all sides of the issues are heard.

2. *Am I knowledgeable about the topic?* Comprehensive research and background preparation are critical parts of successful, effective, and ethical speaking. Anyone can "make up" facts and figures, but common sense and good judgment dictate the difference between proper and improper behavior.

3. *Is my presentation accurate?* Speaking ethically means avoiding half-truths, outdated information, lies, and unsupported assertions, and not withholding relevant information from the audience. It is also unethical to intentionally use words audience members do not understand or to advance unexplained ideas or concepts. Emotional appeals designed and intended solely to frighten the audience must also be avoided. Additionally, accuracy means avoiding

any form of plagiarism. Presenting information that is not a product of your own creativity or repeating entire phrases, sentences, or paragraphs without citing sources constitutes plagiarism. Plagiarism can be as blatant as stealing an entire speech or as subtle as repeating a witty quotation as if it were your own creation.

4. *Do I respect the audience?* Never amplify, oversimplify, or "adjust" the truth because you think the listeners are not knowledgeable on the topic and will not notice the distortion. Do not withhold or change information on the assumption that the listeners, regardless of their cultural background, are incapable of understanding the message.

5. *Is my speech free from personal attacks?* To disparage another person or culture is another example of improper ethical behavior.

The Receiver's Responsibilities

Listening to a presentation also carries ethical responsibilities. Since communication is a two-way process, the receiver (listener) has an obligation to pay close attention and try to fully comprehend the speaker's comments. Ethical listeners also create an atmosphere that encourages speakers. If a listener displays negative feedback (looking out the window, doodling, or yawning), the speaker is bound to become tense or even distracted. Positive feedback, such as leaning forward, smiling, making eye contact, nodding affirmatively, and being attentive send the speaker messages of encouragement. The listener has an ethical obligation to be open minded, to critically evaluate what is heard, and to refrain from drawing conclusions until all the evidence has been presented. An ethical listener will delay reaching any fixed conclusions until the speaker has finished the speech. A receiver who stops listening before the conclusion often misses new and useful information.

The Role of Culture in Ethics

As is evident from the preceding chapters, we have been talking about the role of culture in nearly every phase of the communication process. Therefore, we also need to discuss how ethics and culture are linked, because ethical issues in intercultural communication can often create a real dilemma.

When compared with one another, cultures are like people. They differ on some characteristics but share others. Members of one culture may believe in animal sacrifice as a religious ritual, while members of another bury their pets in animal cemeteries. The people of one culture may believe in a single deity, while those from another practice polytheism. Thousands of other examples could be used to demonstrate how cultures differ from one another.

It is these differences that make it difficult to arrive at a single set of truisms or one code of conduct that can be applied to all cultures. Yet, an ethical speaker can find some moral imperatives that transcend all cultures. Let us look at three of these guiding principles.

1. *Learn about other cultures.* It is critically important to be aware of the cultural background of the audience, as we have repeated throughout this book. To be effective, a speaker needs to know if the changes being advocated are consistent, or in conflict, with the cultural values, beliefs and behaviors of the people being addressed. From judgments of beauty to attitudes about birth control, dietary habits, or the perception of women and the elderly, cultural variations have to be taken into account.

2. *Avoid stereotypes.* **Stereotyping** is a complex form of mental categorization that organizes experiences, influences attitudes, and guides behavior toward a particular group of people. The reason for the pervasive nature of stereotypes is that human beings have a psychological need to categorize and classify. The world we confront is just too big, too complex, and too transitory for us to know it in all its detail. Because they tend to be convenient and expeditious, stereotypes help us create classifications. However, regardless of how much time stereotypes may save us, they are unfair and hamper intercultural communication. An ethical speaker avoids stereotyping.

3. *Respect diversity.* There is a natural tendency to believe that "our way is the best way." This is called **ethnocentrism**, which is the urge to judge all other cultures through the perceptual lens of one's own cultural perspective and to conclude that one's own way of doing things is superior to all others. Ethical speakers avoid ethnocentrism by developing a respect for diversity. From this orientation, cultural differences are viewed as neither right nor wrong, just different. Respect for diversity demonstrates a value for the rights of others and is an important step toward overcoming racism and prejudice.

Culture and Listening

One of the major themes of this book is that the ways in which we communicate, the circumstances of our communication, and the language, language style, and nonverbal behaviors we use are primarily a response to, and a function of, our culture. What is true about verbal and nonverbal communication is also true about listening. Like most communication variables, listening is influenced by culture, and that influence is seen in a number of ways. The role of culture in listening can be better understood with a more in-depth explanation.

First, in many cultures in the Far East, the amount of time spent talking, and the value placed on talking, is very different from what happens in cultures that value conversation and public speaking (Middle East, Mexico, the United States). In Japan, for example, the culture is relatively homogeneous and most people share similar experiences. That commonality often enables them to accurately sense the other person's opinion and feelings without the use of extensive verbal exchange. In fact, they frequently see words as getting in the way of understanding. Think for a moment of the emphasis on silence contained in the Buddhist saying, "There is truth that words cannot ever reach." It is easy to see how these two orientations, one favoring talk and one preferring silence, could influence the listening process.

Second, when judging delivery as a clue to what is being said, remember to allow for cultural variations. Some cultures value active speakers and some value passiveness. For example, in Thailand and Indonesia, speakers tend to talk in soft voices, but in the Mediterranean area the appropriate volume is more intense. Even the size and number of gestures are controlled by culture. People from a culture that values reserved behavior will not engage in the same number of gestures as someone from a culture with an energetic communication style.

Third, culture affects accents and vocabulary. Accents by people trying to speak English as a second language, and the difficulties they may experience with vocabulary, often make it more difficult for the listener to comprehend what the speaker is saying. In these instances, our advice is rather simple and straightforward—be tolerant and practice being patient. Put yourself in the place of someone trying to speak a second language that is new and often complex. This attempt at empathy will usually increase concentration and compassion.

Finally, developing empathy as a listener is also influenced by culture. As you would suspect, it can be difficult to evince empathy toward someone you do not know. If your best friend displays a facial expression you have seen many times before, you are apt to be able to read her look with a high degree of accuracy. An expression on the face of a stranger, however, will be more difficult to interpret. Adding the variable of culture makes the process of reading internal states even more problematic. For example, not all cultures display emotions in the same manner. Among American Indians and people in Northeast Asia, outward signs of emotion are uncommon. Members of those cultures are taught to "keep things inside." As you may imagine, it can be very perplexing to try to empathize with someone without sufficient information about what he or she is thinking and feeling.

Chapter Summary

When engaging in both public and private communication, remember these general language principles: (1) words are symbols used to represent objects, ideas, concepts, experiences, and feelings; (2) one word can have many meanings and many uses; (3) words can have denotative and connotative meanings; (4) words convey only a partial view of reality; (5) words and their meanings are learned; and (6) words reflect our experiences. Always remember that cultures and co-cultures often use language in ways that vary from those in mainstream American culture. These differences can be seen in the use of idioms, ambiguity, directness, eloquence, and formality.

Clarity, correctness, vividness, and appropriateness characterize effective language usage. Clarity is the product of using an effective oral style, complemented by simple, current, concrete and specific words. Correctness results from observing the grammatical standards expected by the audience. Vividness is obtained through imagery and figures of speech. Appropriate language is that which is suited to the audience's background, culture, and gender. Appropriate language is also adapted to the occasion. Effective style avoids distractions such as slang, jargon, and derogatory language. Remember the power of language and strive to be ethical in the selection of words and phrases. Finally, language can be improved by sincere study and conscientious practice.

Communication is an extremely powerful tool that can be used either positively or negatively, depending on the speaker's intent. Accordingly, communicators must be of the highest ethical character. They should know their subject, respect the intelligence of their listeners, treat their content honestly, and realize that they are changing behavior—both theirs and the receivers'.

Both listeners and speakers have certain communication responsibilities that are built into each encounter. Listeners should create a positive psychological environment by adopting a listening attitude and posture that encourages the speaker. Listeners should try to put the speaker at ease. An effective listener must adapt to countless communication events and be especially alert when interacting with people from other cultures. Effective listening is an active process that demands conscientious effort.

Concepts and Questions

1. What are some differences between speaking style and writing style?

2. What specific verbal devices can make language more vivid?

3. What is the difference between connotative and denotative meanings?

4. How can speaking habits be improved? Try to be specific.

5. What does the phrase "language reflects our experiences" mean to you? How might it mean something different to a person from another culture?

6. Why is it important to be an ethical speaker?

7. Why is listening an important part of the communication process?

8. What are some major barriers to effective listening? How can those barriers be overcome.

Activities and Exercises

1. Give a short speech in class providing a definition and examples for any two of the following figures of speech:

a. alliteration

    b. metaphor

    c. climax

    d. personification

2. Have a conversation with someone from a culture different than your own. Note how the individual uses language in ways that differ from how you use language.

3. Use a thesaurus to find synonyms for the following words:

    a. fast

    b. dangerous

    c. silent

    d. creative

    e. clarity

4. Conduct a practice job interview with someone. During the course of the interview, try to self-monitor how your language differs from having a casual conversation with a close friend.

5. List some common idioms in your culture that you believe might not be clear to people who use English as a second language.

6. Sit on a bench somewhere on campus. Close your eyes and try to take mental notes of all the different sounds you hear.

7. Attend a public speaking event. Make a log of the distractions you experienced while trying to listen to the speaker.

References

Arab American Institute Foundation. (2002). Religious affiliation of Arab Americans. Retrieved 21 March 2006. <http://www.aaiusa.org/PDF/ancestry.pdf>.

Gudykunst, W. B. (2001). *Asian ethnicity and communication.* Thousand Oaks, CA: Sage. ✦

About the Authors

Larry A. Samovar is a Professor Emeritus from San Diego State University. He received his Ph.D from Purdue University, where he taught for five years. He has co-edited *Intercultural Communication: A Reader* (11th edition) and *Small Group Communication: Theory and Practice* (8th edition). Dr. Samovar has also authored or co-authored numerous books, including *Oral Communication: Speaking Across Cultures* (11th edition), *Communication Between Cultures* (6th edition), *Understanding Intercultural Communication, Connecting: A Culture Sensitive Approach to Interpersonal Communication* (2nd edition), and *Communicating Effectively on Television*. Many of Dr. Samovar's books have been translated into foreign languages and are used in 11 countries. He has also presented over one hundred scholarly papers and conducted seminars at national and international conferences. Dr. Samovar has worked as a communication consultant in both the private and public sectors.

Edwin R. McDaniel is Professor of Intercultural Communication at Aichi Shukutoku University, in Japan, where he teaches a variety of graduate and undergraduate classes, including English Interaction. He received his Ph.D. from Arizona State University, and holds MA degrees in Speech Communication and Asian History. Dr. McDaniel has taught Public Speaking and Intercultural Communication at Arizona State University and San Diego State University. His most recent publications include co-authoring *Communication Between Cultures* (6th edition) and co-editing *Intercultural Communication: A Reader* (11th edition). He has worked with Professor Samovar in presenting seminars at national and international conferences. Before beginning his academic career, Dr. McDaniel worked in government service for over 20 years. During that period, he lived, worked, and traveled in more than 40 countries. Subsequently, he served as the Executive Coordinator of an international NGO. In those positions, he prepared and presented a wide variety of oral presentations to government, corporate, and international representatives and executives. ✦

Index